The Business Representative in Washington

THE BUSINESS REPRESENTATIVE IN WASHINGTON

*A report on the round-table discussions
of nineteen Washington representatives
on their job as they see it*

By Paul W. Cherington and Ralph L. Gillen

THE BROOKINGS INSTITUTION   WASHINGTON, D. C.

THE BROOKINGS INSTITUTION is an independent organization devoted to nonpartisan research, education, and publication in economics, government, foreign policy, and the social sciences generally. Its principal purposes are to aid in the development of sound public policies and to promote public understanding of issues of national importance.

The Institution was founded December 8, 1927, to merge the activities of the Institute for Government Research, founded in 1916, the Institute of Economics, founded in 1922, and the Robert Brookings Graduate School of Economics and Government, founded in 1924.

The general administration of the Institution is the responsibility of a self-perpetuating Board of Trustees. In addition to this general responsibility, the By-Laws provide that, "It is the function of the Trustees to make possible the conduct of scientific research and publication, under the most favorable conditions, and to safeguard the independence of the research staff in the pursuit of their studies and in the publication of the results of such studies. It is not a part of their function to determine, control, or influence the conduct of particular investigations or the conclusions reached." The immediate direction of the policies, program, and staff of the Institution is vested in the President, who is assisted by an advisory council chosen from the professional staff of the Institution.

In publishing a study, the Institution presents it as a competent treatment of a subject worthy of public consideration. The interpretations and conclusions in such publications are those of the author or authors and do not necessarily reflect the views of other members of the Brookings staff or of the administrative officers of the Institution.

Foreword

THE REPRESENTATIVES of business, labor, and other private organizations in Washington have multiplied markedly during the past three decades as activities of government have expanded. One notable part of this development has been the increasing number of full-time Washington representatives of national business corporations assigned to deal with the varied relations of their companies with government.

The purpose, scope, methods, and consequences of the activities of company representatives have received little attention in the literature of government and business relationships. A reconnaissance of this recent development, therefore, seemed in order, and in 1958 the Brookings Institution undertook a preliminary exploration. It invited nineteen Washington representatives of national companies to participate in a series of round-table discussions intended to define the role of the Washington representative and to explain his activities and functions.

This is a report summarizing both those discussions and subsequent interviews that the authors held with high officials of several of the companies regarding these Washington activities. This summary should be regarded strictly as a reflection of views expressed by the limited number of interested participants. It does not purport to describe in full detail the range, variety, and impact of Washington representation generally, nor does it offer a full appraisal of their activities. No attempt was made to verify the views expressed or to obtain the views of members of Congress, or of officials and civil servants in the executive branch of government with whom these representatives deal. These are areas of investigation appropriate to a larger study of the subject. The purpose of this initial effort was to discover what the Washington representative sees his role to be and not to judge that role.

Even with these limited objectives, the report reveals the variety, complexity, and changing character of relations between business and government, and it contributes significantly to a better understanding of the job of the Washington representative. Despite changes that have taken place in the representative's job since the round table was held and changes in the national administration in Washington, the report gives an informative review of these activities and some of the trends that have been reinforced by recent changes.

This series of round-table discussions was one of several designed to capture the first-hand experience and insights of participants in government operations and others who deal with government. The first round-table series was held in 1957 with an invited group of political and career executives in the federal service. These discussions were reported in *The Job of the Federal Executive* by Marver H. Bernstein. This report on the Washington representative reviews the discussions of the second round-table series in 1958. In 1959, thirty-six congressmen, from both parties, participated in the third round-table discussions in which the job of the congressman was considered. A report of those discussions is nearing completion.

For the series of round-table meetings covered herein, Paul W. Cherington of the Graduate School of Business Administration, Harvard University, prepared the agenda and served as discussion leader. He later conducted the interviews with the presidents and vice-presidents of most of the companies represented at the meetings and prepared the first draft of this report. Ralph L. Gillen of the McKinsey & Company staff in Washington was engaged to revise and edit the report. Ralph J. Watkins, Director of Economic Studies at Brookings, organized the project and served as co-chairman of the meetings. Mrs. Virginia Haaga prepared the manuscript for the printer. Particular mention should be made of the role of John J. Corson, Manager of McKinsey & Company's Washington office, who originally suggested this inquiry into the functions of Washington representatives and who participated actively in the round-table sessions. To all of these, to the participants themselves, and to the McKinsey Foundation, whose grant financed the project, the Brookings Institution is grateful.

The opinions and interpretations contained in this report are those of the participants and the authors and do not necessarily reflect the views of the McKinsey Foundation or the Brookings Institution.

Robert D. Calkins
President

November 1961

Contents

ix

The Business Representative in Washington

1

Introduction

IN RECENT YEARS the impact of the federal government on American business life has increased substantially. Defense expenditures, the use of fiscal and monetary policies to combat inflation and recession, social welfare legislation, and extensive highway programs are but a few of the activities that have attracted the attention of business corporations to the significance of business-government relations. The federal government has grown in importance as a purchaser of goods and services, as a source of scientific, technical, and economic information, as a force for economic growth and social progress, and as a regulator of industrial and commercial activities. These developments (and indications that the trend will continue) have made governmental affairs a considerably stronger influence on day-to-day business operations.

This increased activity has caused a substantial number of business concerns to reconsider their relations with the federal government and to place those relations under the direct supervision of a full-time, resident Washington representative. Among the two hundred largest manufacturing concerns, Washington representatives are the rule rather than the exception, particularly among companies making "hard goods" for the government. As for other companies, establishment of a Washington office with a staff providing direct, full-time representation depends primarily on size, on the nature of the products involved, and on the philosophy of the managements toward government.

Washington representation varies substantially among companies, and an individual Washington representative may undertake such a wide range of functions that his job is difficult to classify. He has been regarded by some as a key "executive" salesman and by others as a

1

company "ambassador" in the broadest sense of the term. He has been called a "bridge between business and government," a "part-time lobbyist," an "economic listening post," an "appointment arranger," and even a "fixer." The diversity of these views shows how unclear has been the picture painted of the Washington representative's job in both business and nonbusiness circles. This diversity of view stems from the lack of reliable information.

The Brookings Institution, in the fall of 1957, decided to make a preliminary exploration of the area in an effort to clarify the functions of the Washington representative, and to set forth some facts concerning why, what, and how these functions are carried out. The McKinsey Foundation supported the effort, and the series of conferences on which this report is based was the result.

THE NATURE OF THE PROJECT

The core of the project was a series of eight dinner meetings at which a group of nineteen Washington representatives discussed their responsibilities and operations. Agenda were prepared for each of these meetings, and, in general, an effort was made to confine the discussion within the boundaries of the agenda, without, however, attempting to cover each item *seriatim*. The agenda for the meetings will be found in the Appendix.

The meetings were recorded, but the participants were assured no attribution of specific quotations would be made without approval. The record was used primarily as a source for anonymous "live" quotes of views as expressed by the participants.

The meetings were held during the first half of 1958. They were supplemented by a number of individual discussions with certain of the representatives on specific points arising out of the round-table discussions.

One of the problems emerging from these sessions, as will be described in greater detail below, is the status of the Washington representative in his own company and the attitude of its top management toward the function of Washington representation. Accordingly, to throw further light on this question, a series of individual interviews were held in 1959 and 1960 with either the presidents or the executive vice-presidents of most of the companies represented at the round-table conferences. The attitudes reflected in these interviews are recorded in Chapter 8.

THE ROUND-TABLE GROUP

The group of nineteen representatives was carefully selected by the Brookings Institution on the basis of their interest in discussing the subject and with the advice of various impartial observers of their work. An effort was made to keep a reasonable inter-industry balance and to select representatives of companies having relatively broad dealings with the government. The conference participants had a wide variety of backgrounds, ranging from architecture and law to an automobile dealership. Experience with their companies averaged fourteen years, and they had served from three to seventeen years in their present positions.

The composition of the round-table group is indicated by the following tabulation of industries represented. The total number of industries adds to more than nineteen because several of the companies whose representatives participated are engaged in more than one category of activity.

Petroleum Products 1
Federally Regulated Services 2
Basic Materials 5
Industrial Equipment 5
Chemicals, Synthetic Fibers 3
Aircraft, Missiles, and Electronics 2
Consumer Durables 3
Containers 2
General Representation 1
—
24

Except for one participant, who represented several small domestic firms in addition to one large foreign corporation, the members of the group were connected with relatively large companies. It may also be noted that there was no representative from the consumer soft goods field nor from such lines as retailing. In fact, the number of Washington representatives among companies of both types appears to be

relatively limited. For example, only one of the large chain or department stores appears to maintain a full-time representative although
several of them have Washington legal counsel. Nor is there much
representation from the food industry. In short, the typical Washington representative appears to be employed by a large manufacturing
firm producing industrial or construction materials or hard goods or by
a regulated service company.

Washington representation can also take a variety of forms other
than that by resident company representatives. Most common is that
by trade associations, which typically represent industry interests, and
by legal counsel, who serve as representatives in handling specific legal
or quasi-legal problems. In the formative stages of this project, however, it was decided to confine the study to direct, full-time representatives who were not concentrating primarily on legal problems. As will
be seen subsequently, since the range of functions of Washington representatives is so wide, the addition of Washington counsel or trade
association personnel to a group of limited size would have sacrificed
the opportunity to explore in detail the varying functions of direct
company representatives.

THE REPORT

A few words are in order concerning the organization of this report.
Chapter 2 sets forth the range of concepts and responsibilities of Washington representatives as reported by the participants. Chapter 3
concerns the broad area of marketing activities. These activities cover
a wide spectrum—from participating in the conception and design of
new products through arranging for research and development contracts, to actually making sales. In between are an assortment of
duties such as technical liaison and reporting on research and development work and missionary selling. Most—but by no means all—of the
representatives had some responsibility for getting business, and for
many this was an important function.

The fourth chapter deals with nonmarketing activities that the
representatives engage in, in connection with the executive branch of
the government. Again the range of functions and responsibilities is
broad, and the functions were found to be undertaken in various

degrees by different members of the round-table group.

Chapter 5 analyzes activities of the representatives in handling legislative matters on Capitol Hill. This chapter also discusses briefly the political posture of the company as it affects the legislative efforts of its representative.

Chapter 6 deals with relations between the representative and his company. It can safely be said without exaggeration that, of the group of nineteen, no two representatives have precisely the same pattern of relationships; immediate superiors, informal relations with the head of the company, etc., all tend to differ somewhat among companies. It was apparent that the representatives themselves are particularly interested in clarifying relationships with their companies.

The seventh chapter considers the relations of the representative with trade and business groups and with various noncompany specialists, such as Washington counsel.

Chapter 8 describes the attitudes of top management toward its Washington representative and his job.

The final chapter attempts to distill from the foregoing an evaluation of the job of the Washington representative, both at present and prospectively. It also attempts to report changes that have taken place since the round table met in light of the rapidly developing functions of the representatives and of the enlarged scope of company-government relationships. This chapter also makes a forecast of the probable objectives of Washington representation a decade hence and suggestions for the attainment of those objectives. The chapter is therefore not only an evaluation but also a summary of the conclusions of the study.

THE NATURE OF THE DATA

A word should be said about the accuracy of the data used in this report. The draft of the report has been reviewed by the participants, and they agree that it reflects their views with reasonable accuracy, though probably none would concur in every statement. An evaluation of the comments made and positions expressed by the conference participants is a difficult task for outside observers; yet the reader deserves such an objective view. However, it should be explained that the views of participating representatives were not verified by inquiries directed to public officials and legislators in the executive agencies and the Congress.

As already indicated, it seems likely that the job of representation set forth here is of a higher level than that found in the "average" company. The representation is probably more effective; it is conducted through contact with a slightly higher level of company management; it is maintained with a somewhat more advanced concept of responsibility and propriety. With this difference in quality, and with one possible qualification, the picture painted may reasonably reflect the actual situation today.

The possible qualification is in the legislative area. A relatively limited number of participants devote a major portion of their time to legislative work. A larger number said that they engage in such activity only sporadically. It appears that a considerable part of the interest of companies in legislation is expressed through trade associations, or alternatively, through counsel or professional lobbyists. But it also appears that a number of the company representatives may have been concerned about the extent to which their activities involved participation in the legislative process and hesitant about delving deeply into this field.[1]

With this qualification, the record of the proceedings, when analyzed, is of good fidelity. The discussion was frank and open and was the product of thoughtful contemplation on the part of the participants.

In reviewing the succeeding chapters the reader should bear in mind the limitations of this report. The data have been taken from the records of the eight round-table discussions plus a number of individual interviews. The report is not, nor was it designed to be, a definitive treatment of the subject of Washington representation. It was planned as a preliminary exploration of a largely uncharted area. It certainly is no more.

---

[1] It should be noted that in the period since the conferences were conducted several of the companies whose representatives participated in the project have placed substantially increased emphasis on their legislative activities. The entire function of one participant was reoriented toward concentration in the field of public affairs. These changes suggest a greater recognition on the part of a number of companies of the appropriateness of this role for their Washington representatives.

2

The Concepts and Functions of Representation

AT THE FIRST round-table discussion and throughout the subsequent sessions an effort was made to determine why companies establish and maintain corporate offices in the nation's capital. Of the 200 largest manufacturing concerns in the United States, approximately 130 maintain full-time Washington representatives. A number of relatively small companies also have Washington offices. What motivates the establishment of full-time Washington representation? Why do not all large corporations maintain such offices? Should more small companies consider doing so? What are representatives supposed to accomplish? Can it be accomplished in some other way?

These and more specific questions were raised throughout the eight sessions. Before they are discussed in detail, it would be desirable to consider the rationale of representation in fairly broad terms.

BROAD FUNCTIONAL AREAS

A succinct statement of the functions of representation was made early in the first session:

> The basic purpose of representation is commercial, and I think most of us have overriding commercial interests in Washington. At least that is why the majority of offices were set up.
>
> Our second function is in the general area of legislative activity—dealing with the Hill—to give lawmakers our views on the probable effects of proposed legislation.

7

A third category includes all the rest of our government contacts, which are primarily with the executive branch.

Many functions were mentioned and discussed during the round-table sessions, but all of them can be classified under one of the following areas:

1. Marketing of the company's products or services to the government, directly or indirectly, now or in the future.

2. A host of miscellaneous activities having to do with the company's relations with the executive or administrative agencies.

3. Legislative activities.

Two other functions were suggested, which cut across both the second and third categories and deserve some further comment: (a) helping the government and (b) seeking information from the government, especially in the scientific and research area, but also in economic areas not related to marketing.

Helping the Government

Several participants felt strongly that, quite aside from their major job of serving their companies, Washington representatives also help the government do a better and more efficient job:

> Washington representatives give government a substantial amount of help, which is not generally recognized. I think they save government a tremendous amount of money, although the government and the public are generally not aware of this.
>
> There is a valuable resource represented here in Washington through which the government can tap the knowledge and experience of business organizations if it chooses to do so. . . .

Some of this help is provided through uncompensated service by representatives on government advisory committees, boards, and panels. Many of these committees and boards have little or nothing to do with the company's business, and the representative is invited to be a member either because of past government service or because he is familiar with the Washington scene. In addition, Washington representatives have been called on for help in finding people both in and outside their companies for government positions.

Assistance is also given on an informal, *ad hoc* basis. For example, in one case a representative's office was known to have access to good market research data on a product in which the Department of Commerce was interested and was asked to furnish such data on short notice. Several members of the round-table group reported that they supply members of Congress or their staffs with information on a wide variety of subjects. Several of the participants felt strongly that it is part of their responsibility to help all branches of government in every way possible, and they regret not being called upon more often. They pointed out that being located physically in Washington they could provide this assistance more directly and effectively than could the home office and without taking up the time of key people in their companies.

Without in any way intending to depreciate the assistance that representatives undoubtedly do give to the government, it seems probable that few companies consider that the primary function of their Washington representatives is to be helpful to the federal government. Some of the participants even seemed to doubt whether they should furnish help and advice to the government, except on problems pertaining to their product or company. As one said:

> My advice is useful only if it is related to my business. That is all I know, and I have no time to spend on anything else.

There is no question but that in the process of serving as a bridge between companies, or parts of companies, and the government, the representatives are a useful resource to the government. Essentially, however, although the function is growing in significance, this help is a by-product of company representation and not its primary aim.

Information Seeking

Several participants indicated that they spend a considerable amount of time and effort in canvassing government laboratories, research activities, and statistical offices, primarily in search of information of a technical nature. In some cases, as will be made apparent in Chapters 3 and 4, this information-gathering is indirectly or directly related to research and development that the company is performing for the government and, as such, can be said to fall in the over-all marketing area. But in a good many other cases, it appears to be in the nature of research or technological liaison not directly related to any present or prospective producer service to be provided to the government. In some instances, this information-seeking is performed by the Washington representative or by his staff; in other cases, initial contacts are made by the representative, and the information-seeking function is then turned over to, and carried on by, technicians or scientists from the company's laboratories. Other types of information-seeking also are performed in the economic and policy fields. But rarely is this a primary mission.

INCIDENCE OF FUNCTIONS

The great bulk of the representatives' time and effort appears to be spent on activities in one or another of the three categories mentioned above. Of the nineteen participants, one confines his activities almost exclusively to the legislative area (Category 3). Another, at the time of the sessions, concentrated the bulk of his activities on miscellaneous relations between his company and the executive agencies (Category 2). Two representatives are engaged principally in both legislative and miscellaneous executive relations. The other fifteen have major responsibilities in the marketing area although most of them do no direct selling *per se* to the government. Of these, approximately five deal almost exclusively with marketing functions, although it is safe to say that even they have miscellaneous and sporadic nonmarketing dealings with executive agencies. A majority of the group (thirteen in all) said that they engage in some legislative activity, although only two or three said that this is much more than a casual responsibility.

The Marketing Function

One distinction that most of the participants of the round table have in common is that they represent relatively large companies, both absolutely and within their respective industries. There are exceptions; but of the manufacturing companies whose representatives participated, all but three are on the list of the two hundred largest in the country. Most of these companies have a broad spectrum of relations with the government, partly as a result of their own size and the size of the government. But the distinguishing characteristic of the manufacturing companies is that all but one sell a considerable volume of goods and services to the government, although not necessarily in Washington. It is apparently considered important by these companies to maintain close liaison with top levels of government, even though many of the government's procurement decisions are decentralized to field offices. For in the last analysis the formulation of the government's buying policy, the drawing up of specifications, the apportionment of funds, and the making of the more difficult procurement decisions are usually done in Washington, or at least strongly influenced by Washington. Regardless of what the manuals and regulations may say about decentralization of the procurement function, it is well to be represented and known at the top. The exact nature of this representation in the marketing area will be discussed further in Chapter 3.

The importance of the marketing function in any over-all rationale of Washington representation can also be gathered by examining a list of large companies that do *not* have representatives. For the most part, these companies are either nonmanufacturing companies or are manufacturing companies for which the government is not a substantial customer. Another way of judging the importance of the marketing role is to examine representation among smaller companies. For the most part, representation appears to be a direct function of volume of sales to the federal government.

Miscellaneous Executive Functions

In the area of miscellaneous (nonmarketing) executive agency relations, the representative has a similarly broad range of functions. Some idea of this range may be gathered from the following series of comments:

> One of the problems is to make clear to my company exactly what I do. There are so many different people who come to me, and so many of the things I do are intangible that there is no way of adding them up.

I think there is a certain amount of insurance that is being taken out in the Washington offices. In my particular case, the staff consists of only myself and a girl. Our office might grow substantially if economic or political conditions should change, and other offices would probably grow in the same way; part of our job is to keep a toe hold here for an emergency.

* * *

In our particular case, one of the reasons for a Washington office is to save the president of our company some time.

* * *

It is surprising the amount of time spent by my staff putting out small fires. The variety of questions is amazing.

* * *

Our function is to provide a door through which government people in all branches can get to our company for answers to their problems.

* * *

Your company has you down here for only one purpose, and that is to provide liaison between the company and the various government departments. If you provide the liaison, everything else will fall in line. . . .

* * *

You are the man who has to provide that liaison; you must contact the individuals in the various government departments and, at the same time, keep the people in your company advised of what is happening in Washington so that they can follow up the leads you uncover.

Although the nonmarketing activities carried on by the representatives with the executive agencies appeared at first to be largely an unrelated group of miscellaneous jobs, in several cases a definite pattern could be traced. Two of the representatives serve companies that are federally regulated. A major part of their job is to follow the affairs of the company at the regulatory agencies. Another representative works for a company whose president has spent considerable time in important advisory posts in Washington. A portion of this representative's job is to serve as a resident assistant for his boss. Similar duties are carried out by other representatives who devote an appreciable amount of time to nonmarketing contacts with the executive agencies. The pattern of such relations is discussed in greater detail in Chapter 4.

The Legislative Function

The duties of the round-table group with respect to the legislative branch are also singularly varied. As already indicated, a few of the representatives said that they have virtually no dealings with the Hill. One deals almost exclusively with legislative matters. The majority have intermittent and somewhat casual responsibilities for legislative matters. And generally they insisted that they are not lobbyists:

> Like the others, I am not a lobbyist. . . . Yet I do get over on the Hill occasionally.

Two are registered, to be sure, but they accepted the tag of lobbyist with some reluctance.

As will be set forth in greater detail in Chapter 5, the legislative work of those representatives who were active in this area appears to fall into several classifications:

1. Watching for and reporting on legislation of interest to the company.

2. Answering a wide range of congressional inquiries.

3. Counseling with company management on what policy and tactics the company should adopt with respect to specific legislation.

4. Facilitating, or taking an active substantive part in, work on legislation either on the Hill, at the grass roots, or through specialists and trade associations.

As the meetings progressed, it became apparent that the representatives play a somewhat larger role in legislative matters than statements made at early sessions would indicate. But much of this activity is either facilitative in nature or indirect. In any case, it is much less than the representative's job is popularly believed to entail.

THE REPRESENTATIVE AS AN AMBASSADOR

The responsibilities of the Washington representative were described in an article in a business magazine some years ago as closely resembling those of an ambassador. The representatives liked this simile, and it appears to have a good deal of pertinence.

An ambassador is supposed to watch over, and report on, developments affecting the interests of his country across a broad economic and political front; so is the representative for his company. He is the Washington-based liaison between his company and the government. Just as national interests change from time to time, company interests may, at one point in time, be primarily commercial but, at other times, involve political or legislative matters, dealings with executive agencies, or top level policy determination. The successful Washington representative must be able to handle all of these functions, as must the ambassador at the international level. Both must know public officials professionally and socially and both must know other representatives (the diplomatic community) intimately.

Like any good ambassador, the representative is supposed to be well enough acquainted with his company's basic interests to represent them vigorously. He is supposed to know company personnel with sufficient intimacy so that he can refer problems and opportunities to them and so that he in turn will be advised of their problems and opportunities. (See Chapter 6.)

In carrying out his "ambassadorial" duties, the representative is frequently called upon to work through trade and other associations, lawyers, and lobbyists. He also maintains close contact with other representatives (other members of the commercial diplomatic community) in discharging his duties:

> The Washington representatives, by and large, see a lot of other Washington representatives through a series of meetings—of the Navy League, the American Ordnance Association, and so on.
> I feel that our company gets a lot out of my relationships with other Washington representatives.
> There is hardly any problem on which a friend cannot be found who can give you some information or some help.

Many of these relations are conducted through informal groups at periodic luncheons and meetings. At least a score of such luncheon and discussion groups stand out, and probably the number is much larger. The groups meet every fortnight or so to exchange views, discuss common problems, and sometimes listen to an outside speaker. A good deal of "intelligence" is passed around at such meetings. More is obtained through still more informal contacts—lunches, cocktail parties, and telephone calls. This is particularly easy since most representatives have their offices in an area no more than five blocks square. These formal and informal contacts are of vital importance to the representative in the discharge of his multifarious duties.

As previously indicated, approximately one-third of the representatives at the round-table conference are confined almost exclusively to marketing activities. The basic functions of this group, therefore, do not appear to be broad enough to include the full range of ambassadorial responsibilities. The remaining representatives could appropriately be acknowledged as ambassadors, as they appear to discharge this role in an effective manner. This is true despite the fact that the size of their staffs varies from one to as many as forty employees.

In many instances, the representatives with broad responsibilities have acquired them in an informal fashion. Their original jobs may have been basically marketing. But by broadening their scope of operations, the representatives have performed a useful service for the top management of their companies. Little by little, the broadened scope of their activities has come to be accepted and encouraged, at least on an informal basis. The process of broadening their responsibilities without a change in their basic formal authority or status in the company organization has, however, in some instances, caused some strain in relations between the representatives and their normal superiors.

RELATIONS WITH THE COMPANY

As will be brought out in greater detail in Chapter 6, a number of Washington representatives appear to have some problems in their relationships with their companies. This situation apparently arises because of a lack of sharp definition of their responsibilities, coupled with the fact that they tend to report to their companies through someone in the sales or marketing division of the business. As mentioned above, regardless of what the original functions of the Washington offices may have been, many of them undertake much more than a marketing function. The bosses of the representatives are reported to be understanding and broad-minded. But there are apparently times when these marketing vice-presidents or division managers become a little restive because of the time and money that the representatives spend on nonsales activities. Although no representative indicated that he wants a new boss, the consensus was that unless the representative devotes the great bulk of his effort to sales activities, it would be better for him to report to the executive vice-president or to the president. It may be noted, however, that since the typical representative has developed a considerable expertise in playing up and down the echelons of government, it appears that he is usually able to get to top management in his company when he needs to.

Frankly, it has taken me eight years to convince them that ours is not exclusively a sales office. It simply does not fit that box. Four different people from four different companies have told me that they have had the same frustrating experience.

Another participant indicated that:

The executive vice-president is responsible for my compensation, and my personal assignments come from top management even though the Washington office is placed under the sales department on our organization chart. I don't think this is right, but it seems to be the easiest way to keep overhead expenses from appearing too large.

The place on the organization chart of those representatives who take their orders from the top company executives does not cause much trouble if they and their job are fully accepted by top management. In the absence of that kind of support and acceptance, the lack of clear delineation of responsibilities becomes more troublesome.

THE WASHINGTON CLIMATE

Undoubtedly a major factor affecting the role of the Washington representative, as reflected at the round-table discussion, is the political climate prevailing in Washington and the trend of that climate.

If you look back to the early 1930's, when big business was the whipping boy, business felt very timid about Washington. They felt that there was no point in coming down here.

During World War II and perhaps before, this climate warmed up considerably. During World War II, many companies established offices to handle a variety of problems involving controls and military business. During the Korean War, the same pattern more or less was re-established. And by the end of that period, the Washington climate was particularly favorable for business.

Representatives said they enjoyed relatively easy access to, and good reception by, the executive branch during the Eisenhower Administration in contrast to the reception that business received during the New Deal. But there were frustrating aspects during this period arising from the divided control of the government. Several representatives reminded the group that with a single party in control of both the legislative and executive branches, the position of the representative might be different.

SUMMARY

It must be concluded that there is no single concept or standard set of functions that will fit all representatives. The variety of functions stems in part from the different interests of the companies represented, in part from the different attitudes of their managements, and in part from the divergent interests and capabilities of present representatives or of their predecessors. The concept of a corporate ambassador comes perhaps as close as any to describing the present, or at least the optimum, role of the Washington representative, as reflected by the companies represented by the participants.

Three broad categories of duties can be perceived: marketing, legislative, and miscellaneous relations with the executive branch. Of these, the marketing function appears to be the most important at present and the most common reason for Washington representation. It is to this area that attention will be directed in the following chapter.

3

The Marketing Function

THE MOST IMPORTANT function of many Washington representatives is to assist their companies in marketing their products or services to the government. Marketing, as the term is used here, is a broad activity. It ranges from digging out potentially interesting research and development contracts, through missionary sales work, sales intelligence, and work on product specifications, to direct selling, including in rare instances contract or order negotiation and signing. In this chapter these marketing functions, as they were developed at the round-table conferences, are further delineated and defined.

Fifteen of the nineteen Washington representatives at the conferences are engaged in some type of marketing activity, although few of them ever solicited an order directly or signed a production or research and development contract. The various marketing activities in which the representatives appear to engage may be broken down into the following categories:

1. Liaison on research and development requirements and contract solicitation;

2. Participation in the development of specifications;

3. Solicitation of product sales, marketing intelligence, and missionary work;
   a. For items bought in Washington;
   b. For items bought outside of Washington;

4. Assistance to customers of the representative's company in connection with the customers' sales relations with government.

18

RESEARCH AND DEVELOPMENT

A number of the companies represented have fairly extensive research and development facilities, which they use in connection both with products they sell to the government and with their commercial products. Activities of representatives in this field have two objectives: first, to obtain paid research and development contracts from the government and second, to find out the requirements of the government for all products on which the company could do research and development with its own funds—with a view to selling the resulting product to the government without relinquishing proprietary or patent rights. A third function relating to research and development involves the collection of information on what the government is doing that may be useful for the further development of the company's commercial products, regardless of possible government sales. This information-seeking function will be discussed in a later chapter.

The methods for discharging the R & D marketing function vary from company to company, depending on whether the company produces or can develop raw materials, components, or end items. But essentially the task of the representative and his staff is to seek out unsolved problems falling within the scientific or technical competence of his firm, to refer these problems to the proper persons in his company, and to see that a suitable proposal for their solution is submitted. This seeking-out process calls for fairly systematic visits by the representative and his people to government laboratories and research and development offices familiar with R & D requirements. These visits are made to a wide variety of agencies and bureaus within an agency—the Department of Defense, Department of Agriculture, Department of Health, Education, and Welfare, Atomic Energy Commission, Bureau of Standards, and a host of others. The contacts are made, furthermore, at a number of echelons in each agency and subunit—the technician or scientist level, the laboratory head level, and the R & D policy and planning level.

In general the role of the representative and his staff is to maintain continuing contact with the appropriate government personnel on a frequent and intimate basis so that the company is made aware of the problems that exist and so that the government people are made at least generally aware of the company's capabilities. When a problem is presented to the representative or his staff, it is up to him to see that a technical or scientific man from the company is brought in and to be sure that a decision is reached on whether an R & D proposal should be submitted.

There are several ways in which the representatives go about finding out government R & D problems, but the general practices are similar in most cases.

> You don't go around and ask, "What do you want us to work at?" You say instead, "What is wrong with what you are doing?"
> They will tell you what is wrong. "If we could just get a little higher temperature, a little better strength and lower weight, or if we could get no creep." From the problems they mention, you can estimate whether you can get in the game or not. . . . Then you act as a catalyst between the government and your technical people, and you come up with what appears to be something that meets the need that can be developed through your research laboratory into a program for their consideration.

When asked who on the staff would go to work on a lead like this, the representative replied:

> We put it in writing for our director of research if it is a basic research problem, or for our development laboratory if it involves applied research.

Frequently the search for a definable R & D problem leads far beyond the confines of Washington to a field installation or field laboratory.

> Let us say you go over and talk to the people in Army Research and Development in the Pentagon who are interested in a "widget" that we produce. In the course of the conversation you finally get down to some particular component.
> They say, "On that one you will have to go down and talk to our operational people at Huntsville (Redstone Arsenal) because they are the only ones who have the technical competence in this area and who can tell you what our intentions are."
> There is no point in sending your people who are located in your Birmingham office to Huntsville to find out about this. They are commercial salesmen and have no security clearance; they would not know whom to see and, they would not know what to talk about after they got there. . . .
> The best way is to make a trip, appraise the problem, and then

come back and say to the people in the Pentagon, "Now I am up to date. I have talked with John Brown and I have talked with General so-and-so at Huntsville, and I am all squared away. I know what we can do, and here is what we would suggest."

It is apparent that the representative in this area must not only keep abreast of what is going on in the government; he must also know his own company's activities well enough so that he is sensitive to problems of interest to, and within the competence of, the company R & D resources.

We get leads, and with some knowledge of the state of development of our art we know that we have something that might offer promise. We will talk with our scientists and say: "Do you think we could hit this kind of an end result?" And we will develop a proposal.

Although few of the representatives at the round table are technically trained, several of them have technical personnel on their staffs. And all of the representatives who are in any way concerned with R & D problems have a good layman's knowledge of the nature of the technical capability that their companies have.

In some instances the problem-seeking does not end in an R & D contract because the company would rather develop the product itself and retain its proprietary rights.

In our industry, for instance, we will not take a research and development contract from the government on a cost-plus-fixed-fee basis.

If the government wants to give us an assignment to develop a new kind of ——, for instance, which is a major product in our industry, we will say: "We don't want your contract, but we will take on the job. When it is finished, we will hand the product to you, and you test it. If it meets your requirements, you can write a specification and put it out for bids. But we don't want your contract for research and development."

Why? Because every government research and development contract in effect says: "After you develop it, we own you body and soul." We don't like to do that.

The laying out of a routine "call" schedule for the representative or his staff to follow involves considerable artistry. There is some evidence that unless it is carefully checked and reviewed periodically, the callees tend to be those who are pleasant and nice to do business with rather than those people at agencies, laboratories, and offices who have research problems and money to solve them. In one instance, for example, a representative (not a member of the round table) was calling on the laboratories and offices of one service to the virtual exclusion of another service that did as much business with the company but had more difficult problems and more money to spend.

Also a good deal of skill is required to know the optimum time at which to call in the company's technical personnel.

> . . . when it gets down to brass tacks, the technical aspects, we either call in a man, or we serve as liaison with the technical people in the research labs of our company. I get the problem to (our laboratories) for consideration or comment, and then it see-saws back and forth between them and the (government) bureaus involved, with my office acting as an intermediary.

Another company that is seeking primarily technical information rather than R & D contracts uses a daily diary system to alert its own laboratory personnel to technical developments in government laboratories. Each of its six technical staff members in the Washington office prepares a brief summary or diary of his daily visits. These are then separated by technical subject matter and sent to the appropriate company laboratory personnel for their information.

Several of the representatives believe that, because they are familiar with their companies' activities, interests, and competence, they are able to save a good deal of time of the technical and scientific personnel of the company:

> . . . you can save a considerable amount of time of headquarters and technical people by acting as a catalytic agent to make the requirement of an agency more precise and more easily understood.
> . . . when you get to the point of an understood objective, then you can bring your people in to deal with the right people in government.
> So I think assistance in guiding research effort is an important service that can be performed in Washington and elsewhere in the military establishment (by the representative and his staff).

When asked if he would call this a kind of advanced commercial function, one participant replied:

> I would say, "yes." Obviously the end objective is commercial, even though the effort contributes to defense programs. Of course we would hope eventually to sell to the government. But before

that there is a considerable amount of technical detail to be settled.

As already indicated, most of the companies that actively solicit R & D contracts or R & D information rely primarily on continuing personal visits and contacts with government laboratories and research offices. But there are also other sources.

Of the particular contracts we have secured, I would say that more than 60 per cent of them originated either with our representatives in Dayton (Headquarters of the Air Force, Air Logistics Command) or here in Washington.

The others came in directly through professional contacts in our research laboratories or more indirectly through a society to which these fellows belong. They come in a variety of ways.

One aspect of the R & D task which appeared to be causing growing concern among the representatives is the tendency of the government to decentralize technical work to field installations and the consequent parallel growth of local field offices by competitive firms.

Decentralization has created a new source of competition for us, particularly in the Air Force, which has dispersed its R & D buying.

Some companies have established offices adjacent to these posts. It is tough to compete with these boys who have an office and a crew of people in there day after day when you and your people travel down only once a month. You find more of these offices springing up in Florida, in California, in Huntsville. It is a real problem.

The round-table members were asked how it was possible for them or their companies to tell whether they were doing an effective job in maintaining R & D contacts and getting R & D contracts of interest to them.

You can tell if a competitor gets one of the R & D jobs that you should be doing. If you miss enough of them, you know how you are performing. Your company knows you have missed them because when contracts are awarded, they are published. It isn't too hard to identify the contracts that you really could have had.

The proportion of the time of the representative and his office that is devoted to the R & D marketing effort appears to vary widely from company to company. In the case of companies primarily in the defense business, the share of time and effort devoted to R & D marketing is very high since many production contracts have their genesis in R & D projects. For the manufacturers of basic materials, in contrast to those producing components and systems, R & D marketing tends to absorb somewhat less of the representatives' time and effort but is, nevertheless, a significant function. Although the representative of a materials supplier may spend less time in a particular agency, he must see many more agencies to determine how his materials can be worked into the systems or program for which each agency is responsible. In any event, as defense expenditures turn increasingly to the development of advanced weapons using new materials and new scientific developments and techniques, and as governmental activity in nonmilitary research expands, the role of the Washington representative in R & D marketing will assume increased importance.

SPECIFICATIONS

A second marketing function that the Washington representative is called upon to perform is to participate in the development of government specifications for products that the company wants to sell to the government. This function appears to be of special importance to representatives whose companies make basic materials or more or less standard commercial products—metals, building materials, automobiles, small electrical goods, standard rubber products, and the like. It is of little importance for companies that provide services or specially designed products, such as weapons systems or major weapon components.

The basic objective of the Washington representative in the area of specifications is to assure that the products of his company meet the specifications issued by the government. In theory it would, of course, be advantageous if the specifications included only the company's product and excluded competitive products. In fact, however, for most items bought on a specification basis, this is impossible.

> I think that most people who are concerned with this specification problem are not really trying to get a specification written that will qualify only their product. I think they are trying to get a specification that will definitely qualify their product, but they aren't trying to exclude competition.

Indeed there is some danger that if the company takes advantage of a particular situation and gets an exclusive specification written, it may redound to its disadvantage by getting the responsible government official in trouble.

It is a good way to lose friends, to write a specification for just your product because all of a sudden the roof may cave in on the responsible fellow. You actually won't be helping him.

A great deal of the work that company representatives do in the specification field appears to be funneled through one or more trade associations. The association is frequently able to get the government office to call an industry meeting for advice on what the specification should contain. This technique is especially useful if the government is thinking of establishing standards that would be unnecessarily complicated or difficult. In this way, too, different but competitive products that can be used for the same purpose can be included, whereas otherwise certain of them might be written out of the specification. In some instances a reconciliation between competing products cannot be arranged, as, for example, cement *vs.* asphalt. And frequently in such cases, the opposing forces resort to various forms of political pressure either to defend their own products or to capture a market from a competing product.

In explaining the use of associations in the specifications area, one representative of a large firm had this to say:

> In the first place, if a large company takes the lead, it can be accused of having a selfish interest; if an association is involved, you have more voices, the bigs and the littles. If XYZ Corporation goes in alone, they say: "This is big business speaking."
> The association may represent 250 plants located around the country, and some of them are small businesses; this is a much more powerful voice than that of a single big company.

The representatives at the round table feel that one of their tasks is to see that the government writes its specifications with enough flexibility. Speaking on this point, one representative said:

> In commercial business you try to convince the customer that your product is better than any other. In selling to the government you can't do it that way; you have to make sure your product can meet the specifications.
> Actually there is a lot more flexibility in a company procurement set-up because a purchasing agent can get on the phone and say, "Hey, Joe, here is a company that has something that is not exactly as written in the specifications, but does it sound all right to you?"

And he may say, "Sure, I have run across this before, and it is just as good."

A fellow in the government couldn't do that because he is bound by the words in the specifications. If they say it has to be green, it has to be green.

The work of the representative and his staff on government specifications has, of course, a direct impact upon company sales to the government. That the company's product should meet the specification is an essential first step in the process. But, essentially, it is no more than a hunting license for orders to be used by field salesmen calling on decentralized buying offices as well as by people contacting procurement officials in Washington.

However, during the course of helping to develop the specification, the representative may obtain valuable information that makes subsequent selling easier, even though the invitation to bid may be issued far from Washington. On the basis of its detailed knowledge, the company may be able to make minor alterations in its existing products so that they will meet the specification in terms of size, performance, or other characteristics. If the company simply waited for the invitation to bid, it might not have enough time to make the necessary adjustments in its product. In the words of one of the round-table participants:

> You may get a government invitation to bid and not know what it is all about unless you have been involved in the genesis of the invitation. If you have, things begin to fall into place. Most invitations on which we have had no prior background are hard to get worked out in the time allowed.

In short, work on specifications provides the company with advance information on future sales possibilities, as well as an opportunity to qualify its products.

SOLICITATION OF PRODUCT SALES AND MISSIONARY WORK

Although many a representative is engaged essentially in marketing work, he rarely makes a direct sale. He may dig out the lead and lay all the groundwork for a sale only to have the order or contract written somewhere else. This fact has important repercussions on the way in which representatives operate, are organized, and view their task. As will be seen in Chapter 6, it also has an important bearing on their relations with their companies.

Again, the nature of the sales solicitation job of the representative differs widely from company to company. One representative whose office is regarded primarily as a "commercial" operation had this to say about his selling activities:

> Our selling on behalf of our company to the government breaks down into two categories. First of all, there is what you might call the off-the-shelf type of selling—commercial types of ————, where we compete on government bid. The other category involves dealing with the government on possible negotiated contracts in the guided missile field, launching systems, and so forth. We are not too much in the latter. We do most of our dollar volume by selling a product made to government specifications where we compete on a regular bid basis for the business.

At the other end of the spectrum among the representatives active in the sales solicitation area is one who obtains no business for his company on a bid basis but generally smoothes the way for negotiated contracts, which are usually signed by someone from company headquarters.

The typical pattern of sales activity is for people from the representative's office, or the representative himself, constantly to circulate through the main offices of the government agency purchasing items that the company produces. The usual purpose of these visits is to gather information on the "where, what, and when" of government procurement, whether on a bid or on a negotiated basis. Is Washington or a field installation going to put out bids for X amount of commodity Y? Where will the bid come from? When? Or in the case of negotiated contracts, what is needed? Will the solicitation come from Washington or from the field? This information is then passed on to appropriate parts of the company's sales organization.

In the case of standard commodities, the sales office nearest the buying organization is alerted to watch for the bid, to be sure that the company is on the bidder's list, and to be sure that the bid can be prepared and filed in time. In other companies, bidding on government contracts is apparently centralized:

We have people who are experts in bidding on these things, and, as you know, bidding on government contracts involves a special technique, completely different from the normal commercial type of bidding.

We always have clerical people at bid openings to determine who got the business, what their price was, and how much lower they were than we were.

On negotiated procurement of a more complex nature, the representative, having located the lead, will turn it over to technical and contract personnel from his company, who from then on will conduct the negotiations. The representative will facilitate the negotiations in any way he can, but the main responsibility for getting the contract will lie elsewhere.

In approaching government officials in Washington, the representative tries to build up a friendly, informal relationship, with emphasis on the technical help that his company can furnish the government. For example, in speaking of the titles that people working out of a Washington office should have, that of "salesman" must be avoided.

As soon as we called our people technical advisers, we found that a lot of the antipathy toward them was eliminated.

As was true in the case of R & D contracts, an aspect of the sales solicitation job that tends to obscure the representatives' exact role and responsibility in the field is the decentralization of government procurement functions to field offices. This decentralization is particularly troublesome when final procurement authority is retained in Washington, with the paper work and routine functions decentralized.

So we don't know where we are. People at the so-called decentralized point do not have much authority to do anything about procurement. They gather up all the bids and they get together with a procurement board and make a recommendation. They have no authority to place this procurement until it comes back into Washington and is reviewed through all the echelons there.

In the past year and a half it has taken the approval of the Bureau of the Budget, in addition to Department of Defense officials, as well as all the echelons up through the military hierarchy. Then it comes back down through all of this chain to the Field Procurement Office, and finally they can say: "You have received this award."

I don't know how much of the taxpayers' money is spent on this, but we are all faced with it continually. It takes somebody who is well versed in government to follow this chain of command up and down the scale.

Or again,

> For example, the Department transferred the buying of stock items from Washington to City X about a year and a half or two years ago. We didn't like it because our Washington sales people are trained to deal with government on government specifications, government bids, and so forth. Although we have a commercial sales office in City X, we now send salesmen from here to cover the installation, which is something that is usually not done in our company. You do not go into another man's sales territory without some good reason, but this is a good reason.

The need for specialists in dealing with the government is emphasized in the following remarks, which also highlight the problems the representative faces by virtue of the fact that his office tends to be essentially a staff office, with only limited line responsibilities.

> If the company has a commercial office there (a field location), that commercial office is not constituted to handle government business. Government operates differently from the commercial field and requires highly specialized personnel who are familiar with government procedures and procurement.
> You cannot just say to your commercial organization: "Well, the government established a new office out there in your town, you handle it." That is the best way to lose government business that I know of.

One way of handling this problem was described by a representative as follows:

> We have a noncompeting deal with our field sales office. We did for a while share sales credit, and they would worry about giving us half of every dollar of sales. So now they get it all, but we get credit on a "good-will account" in the main office.

Discussion of their sales responsibilities led naturally to the question of how the representatives were judged by their managements in the discharge of this function and how they thought that they should be judged. One replied that it is first a matter of good faith. Another said:

We used to treat our government sales office in Washington like all other sales offices, but this office was always out of step with the rest of the company. It is not a comparable office. You can't measure it in the same way you measure a normal commercial office. You can't measure it in dollar volume because so much of the contact work is done here and the order is usually written somewhere else.

A method for determining the extent of Washington office sales activity in another company was described in the following terms:

> . . . if it is sold by one of our regional offices to a regional government procurement agency, that office of ours out there gets the sales credit on which bonuses are determined and salesmen's salaries set. At the same time, because it is a government contract, if we furnished him any lead to get him looking into it—and in most cases we have run it down and given him a package—our government sales department is credited as well.
>
> So, at the end of the year we know how many sales dollars are attributable to the efforts of our office.
>
> In many cases it is hard to divide that up and say how much of the work we do and how much was done by the fellow who actually signed the contract; but at least they know the extent of the business in which we were active, and that is about all we can expect.

The essentially indirect nature of much of the sales activity of the representative can be gathered from the following:

> An engineer in a defense agency calls and says, "I have your handbook here, but can you tell me something about the elasticity of ————?"
>
> Right there I say, "Perhaps I can." I get my book and ask, "What page are you on?"
>
> We talk about it for a while and agree to help him out. One of our technical people and I will go down and discuss the forty or fifty products we have that fall in his general field of interest. They will usually send for several that they want to try out. About that time, if we are smart, we get a customer who fabricates out of our raw stock, load him up with the best alloys, and let him take the ball from there. Many of these requests are unsolicited, and they involve relatively small items and relatively simple applications.

It is clear that there is considerable advantage in being "on the ground" when such requests come in, even though it is difficult to trace specific sales to the Washington office.

Even more indirect in terms of traceable sales impact is the help that the representatives give from time to time to the company's commercial customers in their dealings with the government. This type of assistance appears to be particularly pronounced among manufacturers of raw materials. It was described by one representative as follows:

> We have a lot of fellows who just walk in unannounced and say: "Can I hang up my coat and hat and make a couple of telephone calls, and will you tell me how to get out of this kind of problem?" A lot of business like that just straggles in from Texas or the Coast. These are customers although they may not buy directly. They may buy at several places along the line, but indirectly they buy from us.

The representatives were emphatic that the type of help that they give to their company's customers arises essentially out of the complexities of government.

> . . . a customer will come down and want some government business, and he hasn't the slightest idea where to start.

Or again,

> I think most of your customers know very well how to deal with their commercial problems, and they don't need any help commercially except possibly a bigger line of credit or some technical help with their plant operation.
> But then they come to Washington, and they have a problem here. If it is a legal problem, you can refer them to a good lawyer; if it is a sales problem, you can help them yourself.

SUMMARY

Marketing is undoubtedly the primary task of a majority of corporate Washington representatives. But the function as typically carried on by Washington representatives is at once much broader and more specialized than normal commercial selling. It includes not only the sale of the company's products, directly or indirectly, but also a great deal of what in commercial practice is usually referred to as missionary and intelligence work, not only for established products but for research and development contracts. In much of his work in this area the Washington representative serves essentially as a bridge between his company and the government. From his continuing contacts with agencies, he is able to spot the need for, and call upon, various company specialists—laboratory specialists, technical specification experts, sales engineers, and the like. His success depends in part on his keeping abreast of what the government wants or may want in the future and in part on his intimate knowledge of his company's capabilities and personnel. His role is simultaneously that of salesman, technician, and business ambassador.

4

Other Dealings with the Executive Branch

ALTHOUGH THE MAJORITY of the members of the round table devote the bulk of their time to marketing problems (sales, marketing intelligence, and R & D matters), almost all of them spend a considerable amount of time on a wide range of nonmarketing dealings with the executive agencies. In a few companies these absorb the bulk of their time and attention. Some problems are handled indirectly through trade associations and business groups, but most are handled directly by the representative or members of his staff. The representatives stressed that they often serve as a two-way channel between their companies and government, with information flowing in both directions.

These dealings may generally be classified in the following categories:

1. General intelligence and information—the "listening-post" function;

2. Furnishing help and information to the agencies;

3. Expediting government action;

4. Transmitting company points of view to government officials on a wide range of matters, from regulations to broad economic policy.

Obviously the functions that any one representative discharges in this area depend essentially on both the type of company by which he is employed and his place in the corporate organization. The type and number of agencies with which he deals also vary, depending on the company and the representative's particular responsibility. In general it can be said that those representatives with no, or comparatively minor, marketing responsibilities spend a larger part of their time on these general executive agency dealings.

The round-table discussion also highlighted the fact that the dealings of this type which the representatives conduct during peacetime are substantially increased in wartime or "emergency" periods. In part at least, the function of several representatives' offices is to keep together a nucleus staff, which could be rapidly expanded in an emergency if controls, priorities, tax amortization certificates, and the like were imposed. Representatives are particularly proud of the ways in which they were able to help expedite government work during World War II and the Korean War.

INTELLIGENCE AND INFORMATION

In the preceding chapter reference was made to the manner in which the representatives, in the discharge of their marketing responsibilities, keep their companies advised of R & D and sales leads and opportunities. A majority of the representatives also regard as part of their responsibilities keeping their companies, or at least their immediate supervisors, advised on nonsales intelligence and information that they gather which might have an impact on the company and its industry.

The range in the type of intelligence or information is exceptionally wide. And the means for transmitting it also show wide variations. The office of one representative, whose company is a large one, gets out a daily Washington newsletter, which is mailed every weeknight to over a thousand people in his firm. The letter (ranging from two to five pages) summarizes the day's news that may directly or indirectly affect the company or its industry. News about congressional hearings, word that high government officials are going to visit a city in which the company has a plant, news about the administration's position on a tax bill are typical of the items included.

This is the most ambitious formal reporting job undertaken by any member of the round-table group. It started two decades ago as a typed daily memorandum to the chairman of the board and two or three officers. Its growth to a daily circulation of over one thousand was by request only, and the circulation list is screened periodically to be sure that the recipients really want to continue to receive the digest. No copies are allowed to circulate outside the company.

While there is no specific feedback from the thousand-plus executives and other personnel of this company who receive the news digest, and although it appears to serve primarily an informational rather than an action-oriented purpose, it seems clear that a compilation and summary of current federal news is of interest to a relatively large group within the company. In part at least, this may reflect the fact that, in this particular industry, it takes the place of a daily industry news-sheet, such as is privately prepared and published in the oil industry, in aviation and astronautics, and others.

The same company also has an extensive reporting or intelligence system for technical information, which has a much more restricted distribution. Hearings, regulations, technical bulletins, and the like are covered by members of the Washington representative's staff and dispatched to interested individuals in the company. This type of intelligence function is more typical of the job done by the bulk of the representatives at the round table.

At the other end of the spectrum from the extensive setup just mentioned is the Washington representative who passes along information almost entirely by telephone, usually to his immediate superior. On technical matters he may call or write to the engineering department, but administrative (and also legislative) information is transmitted by telephone since written memoranda sent by mail are considered too slow—and perhaps too permanently revealing.

> I don't know exactly what they do with all of it, but they certainly want to get it. They request a lot of background evaluations, for example, that you would hesitate to put in a letter.

In between these extremes there are a variety of ways in which the intelligence function is discharged by the representatives. For the most part the representatives have wide latitude in making contacts directly with those in the company most concerned with a particular problem, rather than funneling everything through their bosses, although usually the boss is subsequently (or simultaneously) given the same information.

A somewhat different type of information than that just discussed is furnished by the representatives in response to a direct request from someone in the company. These requests range from the specific to the general (from "What was the production of sheet steel in Ohio in 1957?" to "What are the prospects that the administration will increase the defense budget by $1.5 billion in fiscal 1962?"). Because of his general familiarity with the government, the representative is often able to get requested information promptly and cheaply, whereas someone else might spend days writing or calling various agencies or offices seeking out the right one. As one representative put it:

> It saves the company tremendous sums of money to have an office here where they can send a request. We know where to go for the information or can quickly call up and find out where to go . . . It also saves the government a tremendous amount of money by reducing the time and effort an agency must expend in responding to a question.

Except for those with specific sales or legislative responsibilities, representatives were emphatic that the "listening-post" function is the most important single function that they perform. They are expected to perform this function promptly and completely on both the general and the technical level.

FURNISHING HELP AND INFORMATION TO GOVERNMENT

The other side of the intelligence function coin is the help and information that the representatives furnish to the government, either on request or voluntarily.

A number of the representatives reported that they receive many requests for company or industry information from government agencies—statistical data, market information, process information, and the like. And this kind of request, even in the areas where the company might have some motive in furnishing self-serving data or advice, appears to have increased.

In addition to answering specific questions posed to them by government agencies, the representatives try to maintain the two-way flow of information from the company to the government in a variety of other ways. Some of them are largely informal—extra-curricular meetings, luncheons, cocktail parties, and golf sessions, where information is passed along to government officials—information on a new plant or plant closing, ideas on existing or prospective regulations, and the like. Such contacts are frequently backed up by continuing background information. For example, one company puts out a number of periodicals, both technical and economic, covering its products and industry operations. The Washington office controls the circulation of these periodicals to government and sees that they reach officials who might have an interest in their contents.

Another medium by which representatives furnish aid and information to government is their membership on various committees or advisory groups, some of which are organized under the aegis of one or more trade or industrial associations and some of which are organized directly by government agencies. This type of committee or group is used widely in such fields as government statistical and reporting activities where the question is essentially one of fact: do companies have certain types of data, how are they kept, etc.? Committees and groups, of course, are also widely used for other purposes, such as to advise the government on the drafting of regulations. But here the role of business and of the representative is often to represent a company point of view, rather than to furnish factual information or technical advice.

Several of the representatives expressed the belief that the government could make much better use of the advice and information that can be obtained from industry through representatives:

> When you consider that there are corporations that are thirty, fifty, or a hundred years old, when you think of the abilities of the managements of these corporations, and their willingness to help if called upon, there are many things the government could get done and get done cheaply if it would just ask industry for advice.

This representative believes that part of his job is to get the government to rely more heavily on this industrial resource. He admitted that government officials might view some of this advice as not wholly objective, but he feels that this type of distrust is diminishing and that with proper care on the part of the representative the problem of impartiality is not a major one.

Another participant suggested that representatives might provide a different type of help that would involve briefing and counseling new businessmen appointed to government positions. He believes that the representative could teach these appointees (e.g., secretaries and assistant secretaries) the Washington "ropes" quickly, in language and terms that they could understand and in a more realistic manner than could career civil servants.

Although there was genuine sincerity in the acceptance of the responsibility for service to the government, it was very difficult from the discussions of the round-table group to distinguish between situations where the company and its representative were simply furnishing aid and information to the government and where they were trying to "sell" a particular point of view favorable to the company's interests. For example:

> . . . we (an industry association group) spent three or four days at The Homestead with people in the division to get them away from Washington, away from their telephones, and away from the pressure of government, and we had a chance to sit at a round table like this with people who might be new to Washington or who were not informed . . . We gave them the benefit of substantial industry experience on the particular problems which they had to solve. That, I think, is a great contribution.

This representative did not distinguish in this instance between unbiased aid and objective information at one extreme and a company or industry point of view at the other. This is not to say, of course, that the expression of views is not perfectly proper—whether along Pennsylvania Avenue or at The Homestead. But the government official must interpret and use the two types of contact with business interests somewhat differently. There was some indication that the unbiased aid and information was used as a wedge for the expression of an interested point of view:

> We tried to get a little good will by keeping people posted with relatively objective information, which can be good background when we want to get subjective about a problem.

Or again:

> When you go to see someone, you should have something to trade for (his) information. If you can trade him something he doesn't know, he is very likely to give you a little bit more.

On the other hand, instances were cited where the representative performed the aid and information function without regard to a company point of view. One representative told of being asked by an official of his company to try to get the Civil Aeronautics Administration (now the Federal Aviation Agency) to maintain a control tower at an airport near the company's plant. After checking with CAA, the representative found that the airport's traffic fell short of the volume necessary to justify a tower. He was able to talk the company official into withdrawing the request. In another instance, a representative cited the considerable quantity of materials that his company supplied to agencies of government every year for testing purposes.

On balance, a number of representatives are convinced that they save the government money, in part because of the help and information they furnish the government.

> I don't know how many companies have Washington offices but let's say several hundred. These several hundred people are going out every day to visit people in government. They are taking up the time of government officials and are selling ideas . . . (In some instances) we may be costing the government money, but adding all the individual contacts together, there is no question that we are saving the government a lot of money.

EXPEDITING GOVERNMENT ACTION

As previously indicated, one of the major functions of a Washington representative in wartime is that of expediting the affairs of his company through the expanded paperwork labyrinth. Although this expediting function attains its greatest importance in wartime, it has a place in peacetime as well. It was argued by some of the representatives that expediting helps not only the companies but the government as well:

> The Washington representatives save the American taxpayer thousands of dollars by speeding up the rate at which pieces of paper are moved from one section of a government agency to another and increasing the volume of paperwork handled as a result.

Although the expediting function at the present time applies to many types of situations, it is apparently of greatest utility in the con-

tract and contract modification area. The following illustrates the
amount of work and time involved in expediting:

> There is one agency of the government with which we do business
> where twenty-eight initialings are required before a proposal can
> become a contract. If you wait for each of these twenty-eight desks
> to go into action, it seems to take forever.
> If you are really expediting the thing, you go to the twenty-eight
> different people (in advance of the paper), you orient them on
> what you are doing . . . and you answer all their questions, so when
> the paper does arrive on their desk they are acquainted with the
> problem and can handle their part of it quickly.
> . . . the first time (one of our papers) went through it took us
> about seven months to get the twenty-eight initials, but . . . we have
> worked it out now to where we can get the initials in approximately
> sixty days.

There are, of course, many variants of the expediting technique
that were brought out by members of the panel. For example, one
representative indicated that he invites groups of officials to a luncheon,
thus reducing the number of times that the project or contract that
the company is trying to get through has to be explained.

The representatives were asked whether, in their opinion, the expediting function tends to be self-defeating in the sense that, while it
might speed up some papers, it might slow down the great majority.
They were unanimously of the opinion that expediting simply helps
to clear the "paperwork pipeline" and does not slow it down.

The importance of, and need for, expediting in wartime can be
readily understood. It stems from the time compression within which
a large number of important decisions must be made and also reflects
the imposition of a whole new pattern of government controls, often
administered by new personnel. The need for regular expediting in
peacetime would seem to represent an essential breakdown on the part
of the governmental machinery, or currently, a symptom of cold-war,
space-age pressures. For example, it seems incredible that a contract
or a contract change really has to pass through twenty-eight sequential
hands for initialing. The great bulk of these are clearly *pro forma.*
Yet, while the number twenty-eight may be higher than normal, there
is no doubt that it typifies the general pattern of the routine governmental process: sequential checking, "coordinating," and re-checking

by a vast array of officials having a generalized or a highly specific interest in the matter under consideration, but not primary interest or actual authority or responsibility. Washington representation appears useful for companies having a considerable volume of dealings with the government simply to keep the machinery moving.

GETTING ACROSS A POINT OF VIEW

Numerous instances were cited during the round-table discussions in which the representatives had been called upon to get across a company point of view to members of the executive branch. Certain of the representatives did not differentiate between this function and that of furnishing information and advice, although other members of the round table made this distinction. In any event, for several of the representatives, getting across their company's point of view is an important function.

The levels at which this function is carried out cover a broad range, from the White House and Cabinet members to relatively minor officials. The issues dealt with are similarly wide-ranging, from the government's position on reciprocal trade agreements to the drafting and language of particular segments of the Armed Services Procurement Regulations. As in the case of the marketing function, the primary role of the representative in this area is one of coordination. As part of his intelligence function, he typically finds out that policy is being changed, that a new regulation is being drafted, or that the administration's position on a legislative program is in process of formulation. This information is then fed back to the company officials most concerned, and a decision is made as to whether the company should make its views on the issue known, whether they should be expressed directly or through a trade association or business group, and, if directly, by whom.

This does not mean that the representative himself does not meet and talk with government officials. But in this particular functional area the main task of expressing a company point of view seems to be left to staff specialists having an interest and special competence in the issue. These are also the individuals who would represent the company at the trade association level or through the NAM or the Chamber of Commerce. The representative's role would be to facilitate these contacts between company staff and government or association personnel. He would represent the company in between formal meetings and appointments and, through his acquaintances within the Washington representative fraternity, would obtain an understanding as to the position and tactics of other firms or other groups. It is obvious that on broad issues (e.g., reciprocal trade) the expression of a company's point of view must extend beyond the executive branch and include representation on the Hill. This aspect of the problem will be further considered in Chapter 5.

No two problems involving an expression of a company point of view are identical. For example, one of the issues on which a number of the round-table members had been active was the revision of Part 15 of the Armed Services Procurement Act, which deals with questions of allowable costs in military contracts. This effort was handled almost entirely through groups such as the Aircraft Industries Association and the National Security Industrial Association. Here the interests of the many firms were more or less unified in opposition to the views of certain government officials in the Pentagon who were responsible for the redrafting of the regulation. A unified front through associations was therefore feasible and believed to be more effective.

> We do not have any direct dealings (with this office) and act only through associations. That is where our collective strength lies. We are weak as individuals. But when you have 15, 20, or 25 companies whose accountants and specialists in this field are working on the problem, then you get a considered, across-the-board definition of what industry feels is fair.

On the other hand, on reciprocal trade agreements there is no such business unity. Certain companies that are interested in additional protection for their products work through associations, such as the Tariff League, and also work individually.

In the case of the administration's position on legislation dealing with the administration of pension and welfare funds, several individual companies took a very active part, overshadowing the role of the general business groups. Here the companies are confronted with a substantial policy cleavage within the government itself.

In each type of situation, the representative, as a minimum, facilitates the interplay between company and government, directly or through associations. The instances in which he is the principal spokesman for his company are not as numerous.

The "beat" of the representative in pursuing his positions *vis-à-vis* the executive branch depends, of course, upon the nature and size of his company and its relations with the government. For example, the representatives of utility-type companies that are subject to federal regulation spend a great deal of time at the regulatory agencies; others spend a considerable amount of time in the Pentagon offices where over-all policy on procurement is developed. As policy questions become broader and the level at which they are discussed becomes higher, top-ranking executives of the company tend more and more to take over the discussions, not so much as company representatives but as individual spokesmen whose advice and counsel is solicited by top government officials (who may be old friends from industry).

The representatives were queried as to whether their companies have well-developed policy positions or program suggestions on broad economic questions, such as economic stabilization, tax policy, etc. The answer was an almost unanimous "no," except in those aspects of broad economic policy that directly affect the company (e.g., depreciation rules as a part of tax policy). And in such cases the company's position was usually put forward through a group or through a top executive acting in a more or less individual capacity.

The question was asked whether use of groups such as NAM or the U.S. Chamber is a desirable way of getting across the companies' ideas on broad economic policy. One participant replied:

> It is most desirable because then as a company you are anonymous. . . . In the current political atmosphere, companies don't always want to be identified with a movement when they can collectively have their ideas expressed through an association.

Another commented:

> I still wonder, though is it a good idea to retain this anonymity? In the final analysis has it been good for business to be represented through big conglomerate associations rather than having a policy and being willing to state it on every street corner? (In one of those associations) you have so many people that they can't get together and pull in one direction.

SUMMARY

There is no standard pattern that characterizes the work of Washington representatives in their nonmarketing dealings with the executive branch of government. The majority of the representatives have at least some responsibility in each of the functional areas: gathering intelligence and information, furnishing help and advice to government agencies, expediting government action, and putting across a company point of view. But the amount of time and effort devoted to each varies widely, from little to a great deal. There were similar differences in the manner in which these functions were carried out. It seems clear, however, that although most of the representatives have considerable contact with the agencies, on substantive matters they serve primarily as a bridge between government and their companies and company specialists rather than engaging in definitive discussions and negotiations. In this respect their role is similar to that in the marketing area, where they are not typically direct salesmen.

The present responsibilities of the Washington representatives in bringing together the executive agencies with various segments of their corporations appear fundamentally to reflect the very large size to which the government has grown, the broad scope of government responsibilities, and also the impressive span of interests that have developed for the modern, large corporation.

5

Activities on the Hill

IT WILL PERHAPS COME as a surprise to many readers that the majority of Washington representatives who attended the round-table conferences do not spend the bulk of their time on the Hill dealing with legislative matters. For the popular notion of a Washington representative seems to be that the representative spends every afternoon either on the golf course at Burning Tree carefully losing a match to a couple of congressmen or attending (or giving) a small cocktail party for some influential senators. The mornings would find him in the corridors of the House or Senate Office Buildings or closeted with key committee staff members.

This popular notion is wide of the mark in the light of the evidence of the round-table conferences. Of the nineteen representatives, only one spends the bulk of his time on legislative matters; and his methods of operation are in sharp contrast to those of the popular image.

As was true in the case of marketing and other dealings with the executive branch, no single pattern emerged from the round-table discussions that could be described as "normal" Washington representative behavior on legislative matters. At the early sessions of the round table most of the representatives made a general disclaimer that they ever engage in "lobbying." As the meetings progressed, it developed that virtually all of them deal in some degree with legislative matters, although some of them do so indirectly through trade associations or through company personnel back home. It developed that the disclaimer with respect to "lobbying" went to the point that only a small minority attempt as a regular part of their duties to influence *directly* the passage of specific legislation. It also appeared that, in common with the popular view, or perhaps because of it, the representatives regard "lobbying" as that segment or type of legislative activity that is not quite "nice." It is not surprising, therefore, that most representatives do not wish to be classified as lobbyists.

Two of the representatives at the round table were registered lobbyists and accepted the designation. One of these had been assured by his company's counsel that it was not really necessary for him to be registered but he did so as a precautionary measure. Only one, therefore, did in fact regard himself as essentially a lobbyist. Others acknowledged that to a greater or less degree they work on legislative matters, but the opprobrium attaching to the word is too strong for them to admit to lobbying. As one of the representatives said, "Maybe what is needed here is a different word. I don't think it is the functions that people object to, but the word itself."

Once over the semantics of the representatives' legislative functions, the round table proceeded to explore the substance of those functions, regardless of name. The wide range of the legislative responsibilities of the representatives reflects both differing company interests in national legislation and, more important, significant differences in approach to such problems by company management. Perhaps the following statement comes as close as any to being typical of the companies represented at the conferences:

> We have had a variety of attitudes toward how we handle lobbying work. It depends a great deal on who our chief executive officer happens to be and what his opinion is of Washington legislative activity or a particular piece of legislation that we might be interested in.
>
> Usually, however, our work is done through trade associations, and they, of course, work to the point where jointly they come to a conclusion as to what their attitude is going to be. As a member, we support that position to a greater or lesser degree, depending on how our own interests might be affected.

Like many businessmen, the representatives were concerned over the drift of legislative affairs. The companies of several representatives were being, or had been, subjected to extremely unpleasant investigations. They appeared to feel that they were comparatively unsuccessful in getting desired legislation through and that they could block unwanted legislation only with difficulty. Whatever the reason for this feeling, there seemed to be general dissatisfaction among the participating representatives with the current legislative and political climate. At the time of the conferences, the elections of November 1958 had not been held, but there was around the table a keen sense of apprehension as to the possible outcome of those elections, and this forecast of increased Democratic majorities proved to be entirely correct. The attitude of the representatives toward stimulating their companies and their bosses to a greater degree of political activity in a sense heralded the considerable amount of publicity that this subject has subsequently received. This topic will be treated in greater detail at the close of this chapter.

LEGISLATIVE FUNCTIONS

One legislative function that the majority of the representatives perform is that of "keeping an ear to the ground" with respect to legislative matters and referring back to their companies what they hear that seems to be of at least indirect interest. Sometimes their ear is kept to the ground at associations and business groups, sometimes on Capitol Hill itself. This listening-post function is performed by virtually all of the representatives at the round table.

Beyond listening and reporting, the other legislative functions performed differ widely. In general it can be said that those representatives who regard themselves as primarily marketing representatives to the government play relatively minor roles in legislative matters. Among the representatives who do take a significant interest in legislative matters beyond the listening and reporting role, there are several means by which they discharge their duties: direct participation; indirect participation through their company; and indirect participation through trade associations, business groups, and professional lobbyists.

Listening and Reporting

Virtually all of the round-table representatives indicated that at least to some extent they follow legislative matters that have some interest for their companies and report back to management what they hear.

The representative with the broadest program in the legislative area described his listening and reporting function as follows:

> We send in a weekly report on bills that we are following; of the 10,000 public bills that were introduced at the first session of the 85th Congress, we were actually following about 1,500.

Most of the other representatives have much less ambitious programs of reporting, covering much narrower ranges of legislation. The majority seem to place a great deal of reliance on their trade associations and on business groups, such as the Chamber of Commerce or the NAM, to alert them to new legislation.

> Often we will be alerted to a piece of legislation first by NAM, or the U.S. Chamber. They will catch it first because they can follow these things even more closely than we do; and, along with a copy of the bill, we will report (to the company) the feelings of one or more organizations.

But although a few of the representatives report formally and at regular intervals on legislative matters about which they believe their companies should be advised, the usual reporting pattern is more informal and sporadic. A bill that would affect the transportation of the company's product would be called to the attention of the company's vice-president for traffic, a bill affecting marketing would be called to the attention of the vice-president for sales, etc. Usually the company's general counsel is also advised. The representatives who take a relatively passive part in legislative matters generally make little effort to stir these executives to action. As will be seen, only a minority of the group sees it as part of their responsibility to go beyond reporting and extend their role to active participation in company decisions on what to do about the legislation, if anything. This role may be described as legislative counseling.

Legislative Counseling

In some companies, the role of the Washington representative goes well beyond that of simple reporting. He is expected to make some suggestions as to whether the company should take a stand on the legislation and to outline a set of tactics to make this stand effective. In some cases the interest of the company in the reported legislation is obvious, and the company executives need no urging to become active. In other instances, especially on broad economic legislation, the representative who is convinced of the desirability of action by his company must do something of a selling job.

> There are a lot of bills that particularly relate to our product. We are expected to have a suggestion on them right away. If a bill doesn't directly affect our product, then we may or may not (participate). I have no blueprint that I can follow which will tell me definitely whether or not we will be active.

The decision to become active as a company, or to remain passive, or perhaps to let an association handle the matter appears to be made at the highest level of the company; the chief executive officer has the final say, with the advice of the company's counsel and such functional vice-presidents as may be involved.

One representative, in describing this process, indicated that it was often a difficult task to get a company policy established on a piece of legislation:

> The next step is to develop a company policy as to what we are going to do. First of all, are we for or against it? And this is one of the most difficult problems of all—to get the various heads together in the company and decide: "Is this good or bad and, if it is bad, what do we want to do about it?"
>
> The policy having been decided upon, it then comes back to Washington for implementation, and there we also need decisions from topside on such questions as: Are we going to testify? Should we lobby in a limited way? . . . Should we use associations?

This representative, whose company is a large one, indicated that he has to rely primarily on executives within the company who would be favorably or adversely affected by the legislation to sell top management on the idea of playing an active role.

Another representative who had more difficulty in getting company decisions on participation had this to say:

> Many times you have to project what is going to happen to them (company executives) to get them interested enough to pay attention to what you send.

A third said:

> You have to do a selling job on what the effect of legislation is going to be.

The reluctance of companies to adopt a policy on a bill and an active program in support or opposition appeared to stem primarily from the pressure of other business. There was a definite tendency not to participate, especially on legislation that would affect the company only indirectly. Instead, companies preferred to let business organizations represent their interests. Several of the representatives reported that members of their top management believe that "the business of business is business"—making products and distributing and selling them at a profit. This leaves little or no time for getting embroiled in legislative programs, except when the interests of the company are directly and immediately threatened or can be aided. The majority of the representatives tended to deplore this "provincial" point of view, and a few believe that in the past few years their managements have begun to consider their political and legislative interests and responsibilities from a somewhat broader point of view. In at least two instances this wider horizon essentially was thrust upon management by a series of congressional investigations in which the companies fared badly.

But another reason for reluctance on the part of managements to see their companies get involved in an active legislative program is apparently that top executives view such activity as barely respectable. They do not want their representatives to be registered lobbyists. The question was raised why this was so. One member of the conference commented:

> The folks back home think it ("lobbyist") is a nasty word, but this doesn't impress me a bit. Granted they have the right to make the decision; but from a practical standpoint, what corporation employee who has registered as a lobbyist has suffered in any way? Do any of you know?

Another said:

> I don't think anyone has suffered, but that isn't the whole story. I think a lot of this goes back many years when "lobbyist" was a nasty word. It had a flavor of five percenters and influence peddlers.

And yet lobbyists can perform a very worthwhile service to the Congress.

Several of the representatives could be said to engage in "legislative counseling" on a frequent and continuing basis. They regard it as an important part of their over-all responsibilities. The majority of the representatives, however, have limited or occasional opportunities in this field. Whether they do or do not engage in such counseling appears to be related to whether their companies are moving in the direction of some kind of legislative program.

COMPANY LEGISLATIVE PROGRAMS

As previously mentioned, a major problem confronting the Washington representative is to get his company to adopt a policy or program with respect to legislative matters. Very few, if any, of the representatives reported any marked success in getting their companies to think through their policy on substantive economic matters in advance of some specific piece of legislation. Some of the comments were:

The policy on legislation that we are interested in has by and large been developed by my office.

* * *

For five years I have been trying to get the company to say to me: "This is our legislative program. We want to get from here to here in antitrust, in tax, in all these other fields in which we are interested. These are our long-range objectives."

* * *

Until now our entire fight has been defensive. We have been fighting brush fires as they have occurred. I contend that we must have a long-range program in, for example, the antitrust field. What changes do we want in the antitrust law?

* * *

To do this, you have to work with management in the development of its legislative program, among other things.

* * *

I have made presentations to headquarters in the areas of marketing, antitrust, taxes, and international trade.

* * *

I, or a member of my staff, will go back and sit down with the staff people with a working paper, saying: "This is where we have been, this is the situation today, this is where we want to go. These are the positions we should take with regard to this legislation." Not one of them has matured today.

* * *

The decision we have to make is whether there is a basic company interest in a field of legislation, and then we have to develop it from there with the people in the company who should be interested.

This representative had attempted the most ambitious program of any at the round table. One or two others were trying to sell their managements on a broad, far-reaching approach to their legislative objectives in one or another substantive economic area, but relatively little success was reported. Not only are the managements preoccupied with other problems, but there is also apparently serious question as to the wisdom of freezing on legislative objectives in advance of a specific bill. One representative reported that the attitude of his management is: "Why should we"?

In any event, most of the representatives are more than satisfied when they can get their managements to take a position on half a dozen specific issues a year, other than those that directly and substantially affect the company or its industry.

The typical lack of a corporate legislative policy program except in the most extreme cases can perhaps be gathered from the following exchange:

Question: What is your position on foreign trade or foreign aid? Is it the same with every plant?
Answer: I don't think we have taken a position.
Question: So your congressmen do whatever they like. Your congressman in one place might be told, "You ought to vote for this," and another congressman in another district might be advised that he shouldn't.
Answer: I don't think (our people) take any kind of position. It doesn't make too much difference to us.
Question: Do you mean that foreign relations don't make much difference?
Answer: Of course, foreign relations do, yes.
Question: Then how can you say the foreign trade bill is not of much importance to your company? Don't you sell goods overseas?
Answer: Yes, but we have plants all over the world.

Question: Even more reason. At least you ought to have a unified position.

Answer: I agree with you, and it may be that we have, but I haven't seen it.

The need for an explicit company position on legislation and the means for expressing this position to a congressman in a forceful and positive way was emphasized by one of the representatives in the following words:

> The congressman may have some interest in, and participate in, fifty or sixty pieces of legislation, and his main interest may be in twenty of them. Let us say that there is an issue that would be important to the corporation, but which is not on the congressman's list. He doesn't know a thing about it. He just goes along with what the state leaders ask him to do.
>
> You go and say to him: "Why did you vote that way on this legislation? We feel strongly about this."
>
> He says: "Nobody ever talked to me about this before. I didn't know you had these feelings about it, and I was afraid if I were for this, that I would lose a lot of votes back home. I didn't think the people back home wanted me to go this way."
>
> We could have given him a lot of help, but I don't think that our machinery and communications are as effective in this field of national policy legislation as they are in (specific legislation). We ought to have a position on all legislation that has any importance.

Direct Dealings on the Hill

The task of the Washington representative in the direct dealings that his company has on the Hill is partly facilitative and partly substantive. He may simply help other members of his company in their dealings, or he may himself appear as a witness or see a member or a staff member of a committee.

Several representatives tend to look at their legislative activities as falling into two categories: those having to do with congressional investigations in which the company is involved, and those having to do with action on pending legislation. Of the two, the investigations are easily the most traumatic experiences for the representative. It is his job to learn of the probability of the investigation. He will probably be consulted by his superiors as to the general climate within which the investigation will be held—the position of the various committee members, opposition groups, and so on. He will probably be called upon to assist in the drafting of the company's testimony, although this will almost certainly be given by one or more top executives and will be prepared back at company headquarters. He will perhaps also be called upon to help prepare the witnesses for their cross-examination. Finally, he will be essentially the host to the company group while it is in Washington. In some cases this job in and of itself is a substantial one since the company may bring to Washington a small army of executives, experts, researchers, and stenographers. This army may be in residence for a week or a month, depending on the schedule of the committee. Throughout the entire investigation the representative must draw on his store of Washington contacts and knowledge to make the investigation as painless as possible for his principals.

But while the congressional investigation puts the representative on his mettle, it is fortunately not a frequent occurrence—at least not for most of the company representatives who were members of the round table. Work on pending legislation consumes more of the time and effort of representatives who are in any way active on the Hill beyond their listening and reporting function.

The round-table participants who indicated that they are active in legislative matters stated that they work on from five to twelve measures a year. One representative said that his company "does something" on as many as fifty bills a year and that he "follows" as many as fifteen hundred a year. But the more usual pattern is for active companies to work on fewer than ten bills a year, and for some of these the major company effort is indirect rather than direct.

The direct action taken varies considerably with the type of legislation, the degree of opposition or support, the interest and position of the sponsoring member of Congress, and the position on the legislation of the executive agencies concerned. In response to a question as to what he does, a representative who took an active part in legislative matters said:

It is hard to pin down precisely. In some cases it may depend on who else is for it or who else is against it. As you know, you are directed sometimes to be for some legislation that is a lead pipe cinch to go through. Then you have a relatively easy job—just registering the fact that you are in favor with one or two people that you think you can talk to.

If something is highly controversial, then an entirely different approach is called for. Sometimes it involves very low pressure efforts.

Very little direct testimony is given by the representatives, although it is not unheard of. The more usual pattern is for a member of top management to testify, or, if a committee member is from a district where the company has a plant, the local plant head or his representative may be called upon to testify.

I can't think of anyone who has more of an impact on a congressman than a representative of a corporation having a big plant in his area.

Several representatives mentioned that a highly important requisite of management testimony was that the executive be thoroughly prepared. They cited several instances in which top executives of large companies who were poorly prepared had been cut to pieces on the stand—to their considerable discomfort. It was also mentioned that labor witnesses are often better prepared than are business executive witnesses. Thorough preparation and a good witness "personality" are regarded as particularly important in the area of testimony.

But for the most part, the work of the representative in his direct legislative dealings comes outside of the committee room. It is through informal contacts—by telephone and face to face with committee members and committee staff.

My boss and I, not being lobbyists, were limited to those congressmen and senators who represent the states in which our major plants are located around the country; but, as Mr. ———— pointed out, maybe the committee you want to influence doesn't have any of those people on it. So you see a job that needs to be done. You can't do it personally, and therefore you rely on associations, or maybe you can find a friend or a customer who is interested and prod him into action.

Some representatives believe that their informal dealings with members of Congress are of material assistance to the members in giving them the point of view of an important economic unit. In this respect the representative serves as the means through which his company's position can be expressed.

> I know them socially, and they don't have any compunction (about talking to the representative). If they want a point of view, they ask for one, and I have no reluctance, when I am visiting with them, to tell them about the problems in my community. I find that many times they need this help. They may have a very strong conviction about some piece of legislation, but are afraid to follow their own conviction because they fear that their constituents will not be sympathetic to the legislation. They need help.

Several of the representatives pointed out that actual legislative technique tends to vary, depending upon whether the company is opposing or supporting a bill.

> Almost anyone can be against legislation. That requires a somewhat different technique than being for a bill and trying to get it passed; it is much more difficult, as you realize, to pass a piece of legislation than it is to defeat it. You have more numbers, for one thing, to deal with. It is always easier for a man to be opposed to something new than to be for it. That is human nature.

It should be re-emphasized that no two representatives have the same pattern of direct dealings with the Hill beyond the listening and reporting function. Some stressed their role in congressional investigations of their companies. Others represent companies that have never been investigated. Some work directly on at least a few bills at each session. Others never, or almost never, work directly on legislation at all. Of the nineteen representatives at the conferences, it might be said that only five have regular direct dealings with the Hill on legislative matters.

Indirect Dealings at the Grass Roots

Whether they themselves do or do not have any active dealings with the Hill on legislative matters, the representatives seemed to be unanimous that in many instances company field personnel could be helpful in carrying on a successful corporate legislative program. To this end, several of the representatives indicated that their companies urge plant managers and other local management personnel, wherever they are located, to become acquainted with the local congressmen and senators and then to be able to gain access to them if and when it is necessary. The majority of the representatives said that generally their local plant managers know their local congressional representatives well enough to visit with them socially and to reach them for business reasons as required. A few representatives indicated that this type of local congressional liaison had arisen only in the last few years, and several of the representatives expressed the hope that the liaison could be substantially strengthened in future.

The need for some form of corporate grass-roots support, as envisioned by the representatives, stemmed in part from the grass-roots organizations of other interests. Labor unions, the postal carriers' organization, and the Grange were mentioned specifically. As was brought out earlier in this chapter, grass-roots congressional liaison in some cases was established because an opposition group had this type of liaison. But in most cases the need for local support for the corporation was a reflection not so much of the fact that opposing groups had interests conflicting with those of the corporation as it was of a desire to maintain a voice at least as loud as do these organizations, one that would not be drowned out in the hubbub of Washington. Thus the general thrust of the move to gain legislative access through the grass roots appears to stem essentially from a desire to maintain a channel of communication between congressmen and senators and their constituencies.

> We do not call upon local plant people or local officials of our company around the countryside to bring their influence to bear in this area of legislation. This is a shortcoming that my boss and I are trying to change. For example, a congressman on a committee handling a piece of legislation in which we are interested may be from City X, where we have a plant. Well, City X *is* our company since its very existence hinges on us. He may be a staunch Democrat, but he still knows there are a lot of voters in that plant. Wouldn't it be a lot more effective if the general superintendent of that plant contacted him rather than for us to contact him in Washington?
>
> When you consider that we operate in maybe twenty states, that suggests a potential of forty senators and at least twenty or thirty congressmen. If you had that many friends on Capitol Hill, you would have a pretty good entree for any problem.

In a majority of the companies represented at the round table, the local plant managements know their congressional delegations. But although this avenue of communication is available, it seems in many cases not to be used, except sporadically and in case of a real threat to the corporation. Even when the local plant managements visit with their congressmen in Washington and in the districts, there is evidence that they make little attempt to put across the company's point of view on a legislative program. This somewhat surprising fact stems apparently from the lack of a position on anything except the most threatening legislation. It also reflects the indicated reluctance of the companies, by and large, to have their employees engage in anything approaching lobbying.

Another representative expressed the somewhat different position of his company in these terms:

> Somebody in our company—in top management at headquarters, in the Washington office, or in plant management—knows all the congressmen and senators from the areas where we have plants. But our company has asked the question, "How would congressmen and senators regard our (legislative) activities?"
>
> We believe that you could become something of a pest to congressmen and senators if you went in with a position on every issue that came up.
>
> We prefer to have it understood by our congressmen and senators that, when we go to them, it is on an important matter that is related to our activity in their state or district. We must rely on the NAM and the Chamber of Commerce to have a position on most bills that come up. It would be a mistake to take too many positions because very quickly the congressmen would say: "Who do these fellows think they are? Are they trying to run me?"
>
> And if you touch their pride in that way, I don't care how close you are, you are going to hurt yourself in the long run.

To the extent that a grass-roots approach was used, the following statements are almost textbook rules of thumb in the area of legislative access. One participant said:

> I have found, and I am sure all of you have too, that those people who are influential have, for one reason or another, been able to put themselves in a position back at the grass-roots level of being able either to help or to hurt the congressman or the senator. That is a rather cold-blooded way of putting it, but after all there is a balance of power. Sometimes it means votes, sometimes it means

helping him financially, and sometimes it is a combination of both. Labor does this kind of thing, and they have more manpower than we have; but industry certainly could play a bigger part, and top management should encourage local plant managers to take a more active part in legislative matters that particularly affect its industry.

A second comment was:

> I think American industry has a great story to tell, and we have found that most congressmen are willing to listen. But they want you to be with them at times other than when you are asking them to do some special favor for you. You can't be in there asking them for a favor and then forget them until the next time you want a favor.

And again:

> We have found, in trying from time to time to make our influence felt with certain legislators, that almost every congressman and senator has certain people in his district that he listens to. They may be the strong financial backers or the publisher of a paper whom he has faith in and listens to. Usually there is a key to everyone. Our local people, our local officers and plant managers in the area, should be alert to the problems here in Washington; and they could find out, if they didn't already know, whom a particular congressman listened to. Maybe they wouldn't even do the personal contacting, but they might talk to Joe Smith at the Rotary Club, who in turn had the ear of the congressman. There is no set pattern to this thing, and you can't say it will work the same way in each district. It varies from district to district.
>
> I do think all of us have a responsibility to try to get our companies interested in doing something of this kind.

There was some discussion at the conferences as to whether the use of the grass-roots approach could "backfire" on the company, especially whether top management would be charged with dictating to their local plant personnel on political matters. This question was answered as follows:

> The intention there is not to try to force a view on the people in the plants, but (1) to give them at least an enlightened presentation and make sure that their congressman knows that this is the company's appraisal of the situation—that these are the facts, and (2) in the light of this, to ask what he intends to do. The congressman then knows that you are going to be watching what he does, and this has a very salutary effect.

A small minority of the representatives have some reservations about the effectiveness of the grass-roots approach, especially when it is used on a hotly-contested issue.

> I would like to ask this question though. Suppose the plant manager makes known to the congressman how the company feels about a certain bill. Suppose that the congressman says; "Well, so what? The company feels that way about it. Does the plant management, do the laborers, do the families of these people, do the voters feel the same way? How many votes has the company got in my area?"
> The answer usually is, it doesn't have any.

One representative, whose company had drastically changed its policy in the direction of a much more active legislative program a year or so before the round-table conferences were held, described the change and the new grass-roots program at some length:

> . . . it was a very nasty fight that we lost, and it resulted in a bill that tended to regulate our industry.
> We had never had a Washington office as such until 1951, and for a number of years earlier some of us had been trying to preach the gospel of an aggressive program. Finally, when we did get into trouble, the change took place. They reactivated the office on a different basis, and we have launched a rather far-reaching, long-term program. I would like to emphasize the words "long-term" because I, for one, and I am sure my principals, don't expect much to happen overnight—I don't think much *could* happen overnight.
> We looked at our principal competition and at the labor unions to see what they do in the political field and what they do with the grass-roots program. Then we looked at what the XYZ group had. They had one of the most beautiful grass-roots programs that I have ever seen.
> Then we began an about-face. First of all, the lines of communication with the principals in headquarters were opened considerably.
> Second, we started a grass-roots program, which involves all of the locations that we have throughout the United States—all of our plants, our district sales offices, our public relations offices. The program here is obviously, as a first step, to acquaint our people in the field with their congressmen and also to acquaint them with the legislative problems that are of direct interest to, and have an effect on, the company.
> I spent all last fall—after Congress adjourned and until Christmas —out in the field, introducing our people to their congressmen. I

think the best story that came out of the whole effort was the first meeting I had in City Y. I outlined the program (to our people), describing what we wanted them to do. I got all through, and the district manager said: "Well, I can't do that. I have a memo from the company that says I cannot talk with anybody who holds an elective office."

It was dated 1946, and he was still operating under it. This was the old approach to things, but it was still his Bible and the motivating force within the field organization. It didn't take long to solve that problem.

Few of the companies represented at the round table have experienced as dramatic a shift in policy and approach toward the grass roots as that just described. In addition, only one other representative participates as actively as does this one in grass-roots planning and tactics. But although their participation is less dramatic and less direct, several of the representatives take part to a limited degree in operating the grass-roots apparatus that their companies have developed for legislative purposes.

Dealing Through Associations and Specialists

Note has already been taken of the fact that for most legislation many companies prefer to work through business or trade associations or through legislative specialists retained for the purpose of setting forth the company's position on a particular bill.

The use of a specialist was described by one of the representatives in the following way:

> We may be of the opinion that the congressional committee examining a piece of contemplated legislation does not have a clear view of all the facts in the case and that it would be to our interest to be sure that they did have. Then we hire these people (specialists) to visit with our people at headquarters and get facts applying to the case to submit as expert testimony.
>
> Usually when the man we hire goes up, he has two or three technical people, if it is a technical subject, that he can consult with.

There are, of course, a considerable number of law and public relations firms in Washington that specialize in legislative representation. One of these firms was described as follows by a representative whose company uses this type of specialist quite extensively:

The particular firm we use is a well-established Washington firm with a history of considerable success in this field. They are qualified, they are very vocal, they are very careful, they have a very fine reputation for being effective people, good witnesses, supported by good factual preparation. I am sure there are other companies represented around the table here that hire counsel of this type that are experienced in presenting testimony.

Several other representatives mentioned that their companies use such specialists in the handling of legislation before committees to which they feel they do not have particularly good direct access. They are used also if the company feels that an association could not fully represent its position or where no association is involved. A question was raised as to the relative value of informed legislative work done by a specialist in Washington vs. a real grass-roots operation. One member commented:

> I think that depends on the problem. I don't believe you can set down any rule of thumb as to which is more effective. On some of these things—where you have a relatively narrow issue, where he can be briefed, and where he can make a forceful presentation along one line—a specialist may be much better.
>
> On the other hand, if you have a relatively wide-open situation—and I would refer to this————hearing as being such a situation—it seems to me that a top executive of the company, with a row of experts behind him, can do a much better job.

But the more usual channel of outside representation on legislation is apparently through associations and business groups. All of the companies represented at the round table use this channel, at least to some extent, and some use it to the virtual exclusion of any direct approach.

In the development of association policy on a piece of legislation, the Washington representative tends to play essentially a facilitative role. He is in frequent contact with the legislative staff of his specialized trade association and with those of more general business associations. On a particular issue, he is apt to call in experts from company headquarters to help in formulating and presenting the association's position. When this is done, the role of the representative is much the same as it is in the case of direct representation on the Hill. He reports on prospective association legislative activity; he may help the company to develop a position, but he is usually not the company's formal spokesman at association meetings.

The eagerness of companies to be represented before the legislature by an association is due to the same reasons that they prefer such representation before the executive branch: they gain strength from an *industry* rather than merely a *company* position. But legislative representation by associations appears to stem in part also from a desire for anonymity by management and their suspicion that active legislative programs are faintly unrespectable.

A trade association visitor invited to one of the round-table meetings, who has extensive dealings with legislative matters, made the following observation in response to a statement by one of the representatives that his company rarely, if ever, gets involved directly:

> That is the trouble. That is the real trouble. The individual companies look to the trade associations, and they (the associations) are no better than the individual members themselves.

This trade association man went on to say that when his group had a legislative problem that it was handling for the industry, it did its best to get the individual company members to participate actively in presenting the matter to the Congress. It also tried to get help from other trade groups but usually found that these groups had other problems of their own.

One disadvantage of being represented through an association or a business group is the difficulty of developing a hard-hitting and effective program in the association. This apparently applies with particular force to general business groups developing a position on broad economic legislation. Some of these difficulties were described, as they referred to labor legislation, by one representative as follows:

> I think one of the problems that confronts management and industry in general in connection with this labor problem is that we are not united. The unions are all united on all legislation.
>
> Industry—any one industry or any one management organization —is in competition with another management organization. We try to tie it up through the U.S. Chamber or through the NAM.
>
> If you ever attended meetings of the NAM, you would see how disorganized they are because no two industrial people will agree. They can't seem to come to an agreement; and until management can come to an agreement around a table in the Chamber of

Commerce or the NAM, with a unified approach to a problem, you are never going to get strength equivalent to that of the unions. It can't be done.

One industry management does not trust another one because they are always in competition in their normal activities, whereas the unions are hardly ever in competition with each other. . . .

One of the representatives stressed the need to use local or state associations, as well as those in Washington, in the handling of legislative matters. This was, in effect, adding a grass-roots dimension to the legislative approach through associations.

My view is that the trade associations can do a fine job, but they can do it only up to a certain point. They can gather information, disseminate it, and act as guiding hands in these legislative fights. In our industry we have found that local trade associations, or the regional general business associations, are more effective than those that deal just with industry problems; it is much more effective to work through them than to depend on the NAM or the Chamber of Commerce, to which most of our large companies belong.

Although several of the representatives, like those above, expressed doubts about the effectiveness of associations in legislative matters, it nonetheless appeared that it is through this channel that the companies represented carry on the great bulk of their legislative dealings. In such situations, it is the task of the representative to keep in touch with the association's position and its tactics, to assist it where he can, but more important, to serve as a link between the association and his company.

THE POLITICAL POSTURE OF THE COMPANY

At an early round-table meeting, one of the representatives passed around a four-page pamphlet, put out by the U.S. Chamber of Commerce, which had as its centerpiece an aerial view of downtown Washington. Identified in the picture were the national headquarters of numerous labor unions. The text of the pamphlet pointed out that labor had seen fit to locate their union headquarters at the seat of the national government so as to get the full benefit of the political advantages which such proximity gave them. The implication was clear

that here was business's political opposition and that businessmen
would be well advised to equip themselves with a countervailing
political program.

Especially at the round-table meetings devoted to legislative matters,
the discussion moved back and forth between the legislative activities
of the companies and their over-all political posture. It was clear that
the two are intimately related. And while certain of the representatives
see the political posture of their companies primarily in terms of a
conflict between labor and management, others recognize some broader
political aspects. But however they look at the political scene, all of the
representatives were concerned with what they regard as the increasing
political potency of the unions. In this regard, they had some hard
things to say about the political abilities of business and businessmen:

> As someone said, management is naive politically; they don't know
> how to operate. A labor union knows how to operate. It is organ-
> ized and determined and works twenty-four hours a day.

Or again, these comments:

> They (the unions) have ability in a grass-roots system.

* * *

> They have pretty good liaison with the committee staffs too. They
> know what is coming.

* * *

> They instigate a lot of your investigations; they know the trends;
> they are ready to back up the statements that they have already given
> to the committee staff.

* * *

> . . . industry has different objectives. For instance, we are inter-
> ested in sales, we are interested in production, but labor unions are
> interested in people; they are interested in social reform. You can't
> beat that.

* * *

> . . . one reason why corporate management doesn't take a bigger
> interest is because most of them have never been in politics and are
> not trained in dealing with public officials. They are all interested
> in how fast they are going up the ladder, and they don't want to
> take too much time dealing with politics when a potential rival may
> be working full time increasing sales or something of that sort.
> There is just as much politics in big corporations as there is in the

federal government and sometimes even more. While you would think that, because of that fact, they would have a better understanding of the political problems, they apparently do not, and they all shy away from it.

Another aspect of the same phenomenon was expressed as follows:

The statement was made a little while ago that our management people at home are pretty naive about all of this. I think you could even go so far as to say that management is showing a surprising degree of isolationism, while the labor groups are showing a degree of not only national but international statesmanlike interest.

Now, (the unions) may be fumbling for the best way to handle themselves, but they aren't fumbling from the standpoint of the amount of effort they are putting in.

There are a lot of things that have no constituencies and are straight national and global policy matters. You will find labor has a very strong, well thought out view of them. Not only that, they have the courage of their convictions, and they have all kinds of communications media to get these convictions out to the public.

Therefore, when you get into some kind of a public issue that affects us as a nation among nations, you find that labor is the first one to take a position. This should not be the case. We have the capacity to bring out a much greater performance on the part of business-statesmen than labor has with labor-statesmen.

There was, to be sure, some evidence cited to the effect that business-men were beginning to become increasingly aware of the political power of the unions.

I think that industry is starting to awaken to the fact that labor has moved into Washington and that they have no compunction about pressing pretty hard on things that they think ought to be done by Congress; and they make sure that the representatives in Congress from their districts know what their views are.

Certainly management has as much at stake as the individual workmen who are members of unions, and in many cases it has much more.

In almost the same breath, however, several representatives expressed the view that labor is acquiring increasing political power all the time. For example:

Congressional district by congressional district, it (labor's political power) has grown tremendously. Whereas at one time the public officials of the cities and the states were probably the most influential group, I would say that now the labor group is the most influential.

Or again:

> There is no question but that the labor lobby in Washington is the most powerful one in town.

Another pointed out:

> The congressman's office is always open to a labor man. They know what they are doing, and they are as effective as can be. It is not open to the businessman to the same degree. He doesn't represent as many votes.

Again:

> One congressman told a group that for every representative of business who called on him there were fifty representatives of labor, and that unless business did something about this, it couldn't ever hope to accomplish anything legislatively in Washington to offset this terrific lobby that labor has.

In common with most businessmen, the representatives were puzzled by just what could be done about the situation. The build-up of large business groups as a countervailing power against the unions or other groups with differing views seems at best to be only a partial solution primarily because of the diversity of business interests and the difficulties of reconciling them.

> There is so much diversity in industry's interests. You take the (large business group) weekly or monthly publication, its legislative summary. You read that over and it really has very little of any value because they never take a position one way or the other. They will report fully on Social Security, or some nice, safe topic; but if you want anything out of them as an authoritative statement, you will have to go down to their files and pick it up because they are not going to put anything in writing that will disturb any portion of their membership.

Others believe that at least a part of the answer lies in a closer relationship between businessmen and elected officials:

> Some of the more thoughtful people in the business community make it their business to get acquainted with their congressmen and talk to them about the problems that affect their particular community from the standpoint of the plants in that area. This makes it possible for the fellow to do a job in Congress. There is a con-

siderable amount of work done by people who see that their representative in Congress has all of the help and all of the advice that he can get from the plant and from company management to guide him in what he is trying to do.

But several of the representatives are of the opinion that a broad corporate political action program is necessary in both the policy and the tactical areas. In this regard, their views tie back into those set forth earlier in the chapter on legislative programs. These representatives, and they include some whose companies have started in this direction and also those whose companies have not, tend to view the problem more broadly than a tactical struggle with labor. They believe that the program would have to be all-encompassing, ranging from management help in selecting nominees and candidates and helping the "good ones" get elected down through and including working closely with any elected official regardless of party affiliation. The question was asked whether this means that businessmen should get some kind of political action program of their own. One representative replied:

> We had better, or we are going to be sunk. As I see it, that is what will happen.

Another said:

> We have been talking specifics tonight about what the Washington representative does in this area, and that is a very narrow part of this whole thing.
> As I envision it, first, we have got to get our local people interested in our national legislative problems, but, even more basic than that, we have to help people to run. Good candidates are what we need, and you will not find one businessman out of a million willing to tackle that problem.

Another representative indicated that he regards a corporate political program in two distinct segments—what happened before the election and what happens afterwards. He believes that prior to the election corporate management should see that good people were nominated and that good nominees are supported and elected. In this phase of the program the Washington representative would play no part, nor would the corporation as such. The second phase would involve relations with the congressman or senator who was elected.

Here the Washington representative would play an active role, acting as a link between the corporation and the elected official in Washington. Local plant management would in turn keep in touch with the official and his friends back in the state or district.

The question was raised whether it is realistic to think that the two segments can be kept separate. In reply, the advocate said:

> If we should elect an unsympathetic official in a district where we have a plant, we could try to work with him down here and encourage our plant people to work with him at the grass-roots level. Even if he is pure anti-business and has no interest for us, sometimes we might make a dent. If not, sooner or later I would get together with our general superintendent and say: "Can't we defeat this guy the next time around?" But I would not go out and organize anything. That would be up to the people at the local level.

It should be added that the program just described was essentially prospective and had not been implemented, except on a sporadic and *ad hoc* basis.

By and large, the political posture of the companies represented appeared to be neutral or nonexistent. It was the view of at least several of the representatives that a more positive posture would help their legislative efforts.

SUMMARY

Much of the discussion in the foregoing chapter applies exclusively to those Washington representatives who play an active part in the legislative process. Of the representatives at the conferences, those who play a continuously active role were a small minority. About half of the group can be said to have had some role in legislative matters. A few have had virtually nothing to do with legislation beyond reporting to their managements on legislative affairs of concern to the company.

Beyond the reporting function, several of the representatives are called upon periodically to consult with their managements concerning company policy and tactics on legislation. In this regard, they reported that it is often hard to get their managements to take a position on a pending bill and virtually impossible to get them to take a general policy stand on a broad economic issue in advance of specific legislation.

There are essentially three ways in which a company's legislative interests can be furthered: by direct dealings on the Hill, by the use of grass-roots pressure, or through specialists and associations. A good deal of the work of the representatives in these three areas is facilitative in that they make arrangements for others in the company to carry out the legislative function, but a number of representatives are heavily engaged in direct activity in one or more of these areas.

Inevitably the question of the company's political posture, as it affects the company's legislative fortunes, was discussed. Most of the plans for improving this posture appeared to be in prospect rather than already accomplished, although one or two companies had taken active steps in this direction.

In sum, the legislative role of the representative appears to be substantially smaller than might be supposed. It shows promise of expanding in the future.

6

Relations with the Company

AS THE ROUND-TABLE conferences progressed, it appeared that the representative's relationships with his company is a topic of almost as much interest and concern to him as are his dealings with the government. Accordingly, the better part of two discussion periods was devoted to this subject.

In part the representative's problems in this area of company relations appear to stem from the fact that his functions are, and have been, changing. As has been brought out in previous chapters, many of the existing Washington offices were originally established as essentially sales or marketing units. As a result, representatives typically report back to the company through a sales division head or, perhaps, a vice-president for sales. For the representatives who continue to devote the great bulk of their time and attention to sales activity, this channel of authority and communication is not particularly troublesome.

But a good many of the representatives who sat at the round-table conferences have had their functions broadened and have generally assumed new duties and responsibilities. In part these additional duties have been pressed on them by the top management of their companies, and in part the representatives themselves have initiated these new responsibilities in an effort to provide broader, higher-quality representation in Washington. In some instances where this has happened, reporting through a sales division has created problems.

LINES OF REPORTING TO TOP MANAGEMENT

Although it was clear from the discussions that the pattern of relationships between the representatives and their companies was in the

process of change, at the time of the conferences only one representative reported directly to the chief executive officer of his company.
Many others, as already indicated, reported through the sales organization. Three or four reported through some special staff officer, such
as the general counsel or the vice-president for public relations.

The emerging pattern, however, implied greater recognition by top
management of the several functions which the Washington representative and his office are supposed to perform. He is being given
broad over-all housekeeping authority over various resident staff
specialists, who report on a direct-line basis to their staff counterparts
at headquarters. While the representative himself does not directly
control these staff people, increasingly he has over-all charge of the
office and the responsibility of coordinating the resident specialists.
If the representative does not report directly to the chief executive
officer or to the executive vice-president, he at least has ready access
to one or both of them.

This does not mean, of course, that he does not also have access to
other top officials of the company, but the feeling is that the top men
are his real bosses. In a real sense he is representing them in Washington and thereby the whole company. It may be that the president or
executive vice-president hired the representative initially; they are the
ones in the company who know best what he in fact does; if he is to
receive a raise or promotion, it will be they who give it to him. But
although it appeared that this kind of pattern is gradually emerging,
at least for those representatives with broad functions, the transition
is a difficult period, fraught with some uncertainty on the part of the
representatives and apparently considerable misunderstanding on the
part of many company personnel. In any event, the current organization charts fail to reflect this broader ambassadorial or ministerial role
of the representative.

The representative who reports directly to the president described
the transition through which his office has gone as follows:

We went through a sort of an evolution in this reporting activity.
In our Washington department we have three setups: public relations, sales, and my office. The public relations office necessarily
reports to the vice-president for public relations. The sales activities report in a direct line to the sales organization in City X, and
originally, my office reported to sales as well. But it was found that

my activity went far beyond just sales. In fact, sales became a very minor part of what we did. So five or six years ago our office was put directly under the president's office with no intermediaries whatsoever, and it has worked out extremely well.

I don't say it will work in all companies, but in our organization it has worked well because it gives us an entree to talk to anybody in any branch of the company—to any vice-president or executive vice-president—because essentially we are speaking for the president.

It gives us a free hand but none of the day-to-day controls and reports and so forth that may go with line responsibility.

This representative went on to say that despite the fact that the three segments of the Washington office—his own department, the sales department, and the public relations department—all report to different people at the company headquarters, they nevertheless work very closely together at the Washington level.

In further discussing this revised setup, this particular representative went on to say that he believes that organizational realignment has made it somewhat easier for him to get top management consideration of various problems that arise, in contrast to the situation that existed when he was in the sales department. He quickly added, however, that he believes that organization is only a small part of the problem of establishing adequate relations between the representative and the top executives of the company.

If a man is weak, then maybe you have to resort to the formal lines, but if the man is strong and runs a good office and a good organization, you can get carried away with lines. The representative has a major *internal* sales job to perform that will really govern his relations.

Another representative pointed out that a major aspect of the success of the Washington representative in discharging his broad over-all responsibilities is the degree of interest that the chief executive of the company takes in the Washington scene. With the full support of the chief executive, this representative claimed, it makes little difference where the Washington representative comes on the chart. This representative, however, went on to say that an organization chart that calls formally for reporting through the sales department, or through some other staff function, does become a little cumbersome and tends to create problems since there are inevitably times when the head of sales feels that the representative is neglecting sales matters. This represent-ative reports to the vice-president for sales in his company but, in fact, most of his dealings are with the president of the company, with whom he checks frequently on a personal, direct basis.

This pattern of different formal and informal relationships with immediate superiors *de jure* and *de facto* was repeated in many other situations around the table. For example:

> I report to the vice-president for sales. However, I would say I get more calls from the president of the company or the executive vice-president than from any other individual.

Several of the companies represented have divided their sales activi-ties into commercial sales and government sales; this is usually the case in companies where government sales are a significant part of total volume. In those cases, the Washington representatives, espe-cially those who are heavily engaged in marketing activities (either for products or for research and development), tend to report to the gov-ernment sales division or a similar unit. In this respect the representa-tive is thus further removed from top management in many instances.

In one case the organizational importance of the Washington office to the company is being reduced as a result partly of the termination of some financial arrangements that the company has had with the government. Previously the Washington representative had reported to the president, but, shortly before the time of the round-table ses-sions, this formal reporting responsibility had been changed so that he reports to the general counsel. He described this transition as fol-lows:

> The president said, "Now, this really doesn't mean any change. If there is anything I ought to know, call me up. But you send your budget through the general counsel. Send your promotions and that sort of thing through him and keep him posted as to what is going on."
>
> So then I went to see the general counsel, and I asked, "How do you want me to work this thing?"
>
> He said, "Just keep on the way you have been doing. No change. Just keep me advised."
>
> So we have a beautiful chart arrangement, which really works very

well, but my senior to whom I report directly interposes no inhibitions against my getting in touch with any vice-president, or any plant manager, or anybody else that I think would have an interest in a Washington problem. At the same time he does not want to get in between those people and me if they have a Washington problem, but he expects me to keep him advised, and he keeps me advised on general corporate policy.

It seems clear that in most instances where the representative has more than sales responsibilities, it would be somewhat easier for him to report to the chief executive, or at least to the company executive who has the most interest in, and knowledge of, his work, and who gives it its main direction. It was clear that more circuitous reporting channels do not make the representative's job an impossible one, but they do make it more difficult and perhaps detract slightly from its effectiveness.

PERSONAL REPRESENTATION OF CHIEF EXECUTIVE

Two or three of the representatives have a special personal relationship with the chief executive of their companies, serving as his personal deputy in various government matters in which the executive is personally interested. For the most part these executives are close to the national administration and are called upon for advice or service on a committee or commission or for help in persuading the business community of the soundness of an administration program. These executives feel keenly their obligation to serve the government in such roles. Having an *alter ego* in Washington is apparently a help to them in fulfilling such obligations and, at the same time, in discharging their corporate responsibilities. This type of boss considerably increases the duties of, and pressures on, the representative since, like his boss, the representative is also expected to discharge his full company responsibilities.

Nevertheless, the representatives who perform this type of supplemental task reported that it makes their jobs more interesting and challenging, and they cheerfully accept the additional burdens that it entails.

I hope that you all have as nice a relationship as I have in this regard because I prize it highly. This is a very fine job, as far as I am concerned, because of my relationship with this executive.

Several of the representatives mentioned a collateral problem that sometimes arises when a single executive (typically the president) of a company plays an especially active and prominent role in governmental affairs. Other company executives are all too willing to let him become the only executive to play such a role. When he retires, a void is left which the new chief executive often finds hard to fill. Yet in a good many cases the previous chief executive has established the tradition that his company will play an active government role, and it is expected that the tradition will be continued.

TITLES AND STATUS

The titles of the round-table participants cover a broad spectrum. Several are vice-presidents; others are called "managers"; others are "directors" or "executive directors." About a quarter are corporate officers; in several cases this is largely a matter of convenience for the signing of papers and legal documents, rather than a designation of the relative importance of the Washington operation.

There seems to be little correlation between the breadth of the duties performed by a representative and his title. One who is a vice-president confines his attention to sales activities. Several of those designated "managers" or "directors" cover a wide range of functions. Titles appear to be influenced more by the hierarchy of titles in other parts of the company than by the scope and responsibilities of the Washington office.

Although agreeing that title is not really a matter of great importance, several of the representatives feel that an upgrading in title might increase their effectiveness somewhat.

I think the head man of the Washington office of any company should be an official of the company because the people he contacts and confers with are at the executive level.

For example, a General or an Admiral, is really a vice-president. A man going in to confer at that top echelon should be an official with the same stature.

FAMILIARITY WITH THE COMPANY

But it was apparent that regardless of title, organization chart, and relations with the chief executive officer, the bulk of the contacts that the representative has with his company lies with a wide range of company personnel, in both line and staff positions, who have some interest in, or need for, dealings with the government. For those representatives who are essentially sales oriented, a good many of these contacts, quite naturally, tend to be with headquarters or field sales people. But in view of the nature of the service and advisory functions that the Washington office performs, the representatives are also brought into contact with engineering and R & D personnel. In several cases the representative also has frequent dealings with the public relations and legal staffs.

Most of the representatives indicated that they have complete freedom to contact anyone in their companies, provided they keep their bosses at least generally informed. And it is the effectiveness of these contacts that largely determines the success of the representative's job.

A large majority of the representatives feel that an intimate knowledge of the company, its personnel, and its internal operations is essential for a Washington representative. Without this familiarity, they feel he would not know where to turn in the company, would not know the interests and capabilities of the various parts of his company, and would not be familiar with the "politics" of the corporation. They further feel that this type of familiarity would be enjoyed only by a man picked from within the company. The converse is also true—people in the company know the representative and have faith in him. When they have government problems, they naturally turn to him.

I think it is very important that the individual should know his company from within and be known from within before he takes on a job of this sort because of the broad diversification of contacts. This is true especially in a company of our size with operations all over the country.

We have to know the people who run all these different divisions, and I think it is important that we be given sufficient stature, attend the right staff meetings, and mix socially with the right group in the corporation so we are accepted as one of them.

We can't be treated as outsiders and expect to be brought into these problems the way we should be. I think it is very important—in fact, I put it almost number one as a requisite—for a man in Washington to know the company he is going to represent.

Another aspect of the need for familiarity with the company concerns familiarity with its product.

It is not nearly so essential for a person to have grown up in a company if he is representing a company with limited products. Let us say a smaller company rather than one of the large billion dollar corporations with ten thousand products.

At the last count our company had something like 16,000 products. You couldn't possibly acquire familiarity with those products overnight. We fellows in Washington are not specialists on any of these multi-thousand products, but we all know something about every one of them.

Although there were some dissenters from the view that the Washington representative should usually, or always, be an inside man, there was virtual unanimity that he should know his company's products thoroughly if he had any appreciable sales responsibility.

One large company, in looking for a candidate who would eventually replace their current representative, selected an inside man with approximately fifteen years in the company, during which time he had moved a considerable number of times not only geographically, but also from department to department. It was generally agreed within the company that he would be allowed at least five years to get thoroughly acquainted with the Washington scene.

One representative vigorously dissented from the view that the ideal representative should be a company man.

If you want to talk exclusively in terms of sales instead of Washington representation (which is a whole series of things), I agree with you. If a man is going to sell my product, I want him to know what the product is.

But if you are going to cover the whole range of Washington activities, then I think you can ask, "Am I better off having a man who has lived in the steel industry or the rubber industry or the Y industry, or am I better off having a man who has lived in the Washington industry?"

You can argue one way or the other. There are things to be said on both sides. But the man who really knows Washington, who knows government people, how they think, what impresses them, and what doesn't impress them, will do a fine job.

As though to echo this thought and illustrate the dilemma, one representative who spoke vigorously of the desirability of having an "inside" man (and who was one himself) had recently hired a potential replacement who had had long experience in government. This neophyte was being given a detailed "course" in the company that he might someday represent.

THE RANGE OF CONTACTS

The very broad range of contacts which the representatives have with one part of their companies or another can perhaps best be indicated by the following descriptions given at the round-table sessions. A representative who concentrated on legislative matters had this to say:

A bill was introduced having to do with the importation of exhibition products—products imported from abroad for show purposes in the United States. Passage of this bill was of direct interest to the company.

I spent considerable time on this bill even though in dollars it is not very important. I think I talked to one person at headquarters, someone in the legal department that I called on for help. He was the only one back there who knows that the bill has passed unless someone else is watching the report closely, but I worked on that bill because it had an effect. I talked to the congressman who introduced it, and I helped get the bill passed. It was not controversial. Then you move from something like that to something like the Senate investigation where there is no bill introduced but we spend hundreds of thousands of dollars in man-hours preparing for and testifying on it—the follow-up and everything that goes with a major hearing. For something like that, of course, I am in close contact with dozens of people in the company.

Another representative whose duties were oriented primarily toward sales and technical service spoke of his company dealings as follows:

Let's put it this way: We find it easier for the four of us in the office to report directly. We are all experienced people in the company. We think that it isn't good to put an inexperienced person in Washington, so we hire very few people here. It must be somebody who has had quite a background in the company. Knowing his way around, he reports the various things that he runs into directly to the interested department for action.

These actions may be something in connection with a public opening of a bid, something to do with negotiations, something to do with a wild question out of the blue that some government department wants an answer to. It may have to do with a research or development item.

My boys pretty generally know where to go. They lean on me for new items with which they have had no previous experience; and these things happen in Washington every few days. They come to me and say, "Here is the problem. What should I do with it?" I may handle that myself, or I may suggest to them that they handle it with "X" person in "X" department at some division of the company.

We do have access and private lines to every division of our company, and we can go direct to any division for answers or for action and for assistance. We call for assistance many times. We have no permanent technical staff here, and a lot of our work is of a technical nature, so we have to call on the division for our first-hand technical information. Their people come in here and work with our people, who establish the contacts and who expose our technicians to the technical problems and to government technical personnel.

The person in our company who is charged with governmental relations is our executive vice-president. He controls my salary and would control my promotion although there isn't much promotion from Washington. You would have to move out of here if you were going to be promoted in our setup.

However, while I send, I would say, half of my reports directly to him, organizationally I am not directly under him but under the division director two echelons down.

And another representative primarily sales oriented said:

I report to these two (division) vice-presidents. I am at perfect liberty to, and do, talk to many others above and below them in the organization. It is a two-way street. In fact, I get too many of these calls at home at midnight or thereabouts, but we do pride ourselves on having what we feel are very close ties with these groups, close cooperation with them and very good lines of communications.

A representative who has much broader functions, and who maintains that he does not engage in sales activities said:

Now, apart from what I initiate myself, I get requests from all over my company to do things. You can go to purchasing, or sales or promotion, or any one of these divisions, and if anybody asks the man at the top there if I am important, he will say, "Hell, no, he never does anything for me."

But, if you move down one layer, or two layers—and I have just checked this and that is how I happen to know—this month I have done nine different things in connection with sales, which range from something that is relatively unimportant to something that is very important.

But to find out what I do in my company you would have to talk to 100 or 150 different people. No one person knows or could know.

It is clear from these excerpts—and they were echoed and re-echoed throughout the round-table sessions—that the Washington representative must deal with virtually all echelons and all functional areas within his company. This is true regardless of formal organizational charts, titles, lines of reporting, or anything else. Since he is at once of assistance to the various staff and line units of his company and also the recipient of their assistance, it is clear that his success is absolutely dependent upon his building up good working relations with a broad spectrum of company personnel and that he must hold their confidence. This does not mean that a representative can afford to neglect his governmental relations, but it is to say that, to capitalize fully on his expertise in moving about the Washington scene, he must keep in close touch with the "folks back home." Clarity of authority, title, intimate familiarity with company products and policies, good relations with the chief executive, all contribute to the establishment and maintenance of good relations with the company. But, in the last analysis, it appears that the maintenance of these relations rests primarily on personal contacts (often by telephone) between the representative and company personnel.

REPORTING AND COMMUNICATION

Most of the representatives at the round tables indicated that part of their program of keeping in close touch with the company is a series of reports and more informal communications. Some of these are more or less formal monthly or quarterly reports to one or more individuals in the company. These typically give a resumé or summary of the representative's activities for the preceding period and are designed to keep the recipients up to date with the Washington scene. At the other extreme is the representative who files no formal written reports, but who is on the phone to his boss and others in the company two or three times a day via private wire. The use of carbon "information" copies appears to be widespread. In part these are carbons of reports or memoranda to the representative's boss, which he sends to others; in part they are carbons of memoranda to others, which the representative furnishes his boss for coordination and information purposes. Since, as has already been mentioned, most of the representatives have authority to contact anyone in the company, without going through channels, these carbon copies serve to keep the representatives' activities in channels *ex post facto*.

One representative who does not make systematic reports indicated that while the round tables were in progress, his company management was questioning the need for a Washington office.

> In my company two weeks ago a question was raised about the Washington office—just what we are studying here. Does the Washington office produce? One man thinks it doesn't produce. Why does he think so? Because he doesn't know what I have been doing. I haven't been reporting to him. That is where I have made a mistake.
>
> The president of the company, on the other hand, feels instinctively that he ought to have a Washington office. But he doesn't know what I do either, so how can he argue with this other man, my boss, the vice-president? In the last two weeks I have been trying to figure out what I contribute to the company. I have compiled a long report about what I have been doing in the last six years.
>
> The president of my company knows instinctively that if he has a billion dollar business and if the government is as large as it is, and if you have the kind of international situation that we have, then he has an obligation and a responsibility to keep in touch with governmental affairs. But he also has to live with his stockholders, and if he is spending money on things that aren't profitable, he is not doing a good job, so he has to look at profit and loss. If I can't show him some contribution to profit, he ought to close the place up. But I am convinced that you not only have to look at the tangibles; I think you have to get into the intangibles as well.

The consensus of the representatives seemed to be that while formal reports take time to prepare and have often been outdated by events by the time they reach their addressees, they nevertheless serve a useful purpose in providing a running record of the varied activities of the representatives.

Although written and telephonic communications appear to constitute the bulk of the contacts that representatives have with company personnel, there is also a great deal of face-to-face contact. Much of this occurs in Washington when company personnel come to town. Most of the representatives reported that they have a fairly steady stream of company visitors ranging from top executives on down. The pattern of these visits depends primarily on the amount and type of dealings that the company has with the government. The president of one company whose representative attended the round tables comes to Washington almost weekly. The president of another company almost never comes to Washington, but his company usually has several sales engineers, R & D personnel, and others in town. The representatives were unanimous in saying that they like to have all company personnel who visit Washington clear through their offices, regardless of whether they themselves are directly involved in the matter on which the visitor is engaged. In a good many cases clearing through the Washington office is a matter of routine convenience since this office makes hotel accommodations and appointments, provides a message center, and generally facilitates the trip of the company man. Failure to check through the Washington office, it was agreed, often results in unnecessary trips to Washington or in an embarrassing lack of coordination of visits in the agencies.

A few of the representatives make frequent trips to company headquarters or to company installations. At the other extreme, a few representatives almost never "go home." One said:

> I haven't been back to X in two and a half years. Actually, I am very fortunate in that almost all of our top people at one time or another come here. They are happy to discuss their problem right on the ground, and they come so frequently I don't have to go to X.

Another commented:

> I have seen periods of as much as six months go by without my being in the home office. More recently, I have been going up about once a month.

A third said:

> I might go (to headquarters) once a week for a month then not
> be there for six or eight months. I do what the occasion demands.

SUMMARY

It is apparent from the foregoing description of the relations that
representatives maintain with their companies that no standard pattern of relations is followed. Nor is it possible to lay down any hard
and fast rules for an ideal relationship. The appropriateness of any
particular set of relations must be gauged primarily by the tasks and
functions that the company wants the representative to perform and
that he in fact does perform. If he is primarily marketing-oriented,
there seems to be no doubt that he can satisfactorily report to the top
marketing officials and, with due regard to the peculiar nature of
marketing to the government, can conduct his company relations on
more or less the same lines as a regional or product sales office or
division. It goes without saying that, in this capacity, the closer his
ties are with the sales staff and with other parts of the company that
shape the product or service, the more effective he can be.

As the responsibilities of the representative begin to broaden out
beyond the marketing area, then his relations with the company become more complex. If a major share of his time and effort is directed
toward nonmarketing activity, then a channel into the company
through the sales or marketing organization may begin to cause some
friction or lack of understanding. Where the representative is, in fact,
a company ambassador or where he is dealing with top policy matters,
it would seem to be preferable to have him report, both *de jure* and
de facto, to top management. Although it is true that reporting
through sales or some other functional department does not appear to
impede the representative from moving around within the company,
the round-table conversations revealed a certain amount of concern
on the part of those representatives whose lines of communication and
authority are ambiguous.

There is no doubt that the interest of top management in government affairs strongly affects the role and effectiveness of the repre-

sentative's work, particularly in over-all, ambassadorial-type representation. Particularly in recent years, a part of the task of the representative has consisted in helping to focus the attention of top management on long-run government economic policies that might affect his company. At both the legislative and the executive level, following and participating in the formulation of such policies is coming to be regarded more and more as an integral part of the representative's task. Whether this type of company interest in economic policies would be the same under a different type of administration and in a different type of legislative climate cannot be accurately forecast. It seems likely, however, that efforts of large companies to have a voice in the shaping of such policies will be a continuing phenomenon. As a result, the status and reporting relationships of Washington representatives may take on added significance.

7

Relations with Groups and Washington Specialists

RELATIONSHIPS BETWEEN government and business are maintained by other organizations and individuals in addition to company Washington representatives. Other bridges are provided by a multitude of groups and associations and by various types of specialists—lawyers, lobbyists, and public relations specialists. Therefore, it seemed desirable to the participants to explore the relations existing between company representatives on the one hand and groups, associations, and specialists on the other.

GROUPS AND ASSOCIATIONS

The discussions were directed to several categories of groups and associations: general purpose business groups, special purpose groups, trade associations, and "all other" groups.

General Purpose Groups

The consensus of the round table was that while substantial improvement is being made in the work of the general business organizations, they are not wholly satisfactory either as an aid to the representative in carrying out his functions, or to his firm or the business community as spokesmen for business. They complained that the membership of the general purpose groups is so broad, and the interests of the individual members so diverse, that the positions of the groups are watered down excessively and, once taken, are too inflexible for the give-and-take of the Washington environment. Thus, it was claimed, the groups find it difficult to maneuver adequately.

The representatives, however, do tend to look to these general organizations for a variety of different functions. Some use them as sources of detailed information on matters that the representatives themselves are not actively working on. Others look to them for general briefings on such subjects as legislation, agricultural policy, social security, pension funds, and the like. Still others use them as a repository for problems which they themselves do not have time to handle.

The area of legislative "briefings" is apparently a relatively new field. One representative spoke of the program, which is especially designed for Washington representatives and trade association officials, as follows:

I think the staff gave the best briefings on the legislative picture that I have ever heard. They have had four of them since they started their new program, and they have been really wonderful.

In my case, I follow certain kinds of legislation. I don't follow the whole field, as perhaps some people do. The organization did a fine job of bringing people up-to-date and keeping them up-to-date.

On the level of somewhat more specific information, one representative had the following to say:

They have a little luncheon group that has met weekly for years, with a lot of different industries in the over-all building and construction field represented. They usually have a key speaker from the Hill or from some department of government.

I attend about every other Friday, depending on the speaker. There are, I suppose, about forty companies represented and also a lot of trade associations.

I find that it is a very good meeting ground and quite a refresher and that there are a number of people at these meetings who are interested in what others are doing. I believe that this is very helpful.

With reference to more technical information, a number of the representatives indicated that they rely extensively on individual staff members of the general organizations. And this is in spite of the fact that these same representatives feel that those groups are largely ineffective in the legislative area. Asked whether the staffs are of any help as sources of information, one representative replied:

> The specialists on their staffs are. They have a man over there who spends all of his time on _____ law and _____ problems, and if I really want to know what is going on and I have been away from it, I can call this man and in ten minutes get really good information.

Several of the representatives indicated that they use the general business organizations to handle problems that the representative or his company cannot cover adequately.

> My interest is more in trying to hand over to them those problems of a very general business legislative nature that we don't have the personnel to handle ourselves.
>
> One of the problems we have been interested in is the changes in the Social Security and pension fund laws. Those are issues that we just don't have the people to cover in our company. But we have found that the general organizations can do a pretty fair job in an over-all way that we would be prepared to endorse.
>
> We watch what they are trying to do. We try to help them if we can, but we can pretty well mark a problem off our list of things to work on if they are working on it. We just don't have to follow it in detail.

Although the representatives had some nice things to say about the general business groups and especially about the technical capabilities of their staffs, several voiced dissatisfaction with both groups as over-extended, lacking in leadership, and ineffective in translating their programs into legislation.

> At the grass-roots level there is much that needs to be done, and they have done a lot in terms of the business environment. But if you translate this into legislative effort, you find they have fallen down badly.
>
> They are so big that it is virtually impossible for them to reach a unanimous view on any controversial subject. Take a subject that is not too controversial in business, such as taxation—a principle in taxation—the positions they have taken on the Hill have been so reactionary that they have lost all respect, literally all respect, of the lawmakers.

Recent improvement in performance was noted, but, as one partici-pant asked, "Aren't we essentially damning these groups with faint praise?" A number of representatives pointed out that the problems of these large general organizations had been partially responsible for the rise of some smaller general purpose groups which focus specifically on legislative action and for the programs of many trade associations and federations of trade associations.

> . . . the strength of these other groups has come from the fact that the larger general organizations have been unable to fulfill the need.

Toward the end of the discussion on these general purpose groups, one member of the round table raised the question whether membership in such groups is not essentially a retreat from responsible action by businessmen and firms.

> . . . will they default on any further interest in, or responsibility for, a particular issue, feeling that by being a member of an association they have someone else looking out for them? I am not settled in my own mind that this happens, but I suspect that in many cases it does.

In the discussions that followed, this charge was expanded to include the possibility that the general purpose groups might even serve as a barrier to the flow of information on the realities of Washington to individual business leaders.

Not more than a handful of the representatives felt this strongly about the matter, but there was general dissatisfaction with these organizations as spokesmen for business and as lobbyists for legislation favorable to business.

> It is unlikely that many of us would be here if these organizations and our trade associations had done a completely effective and thorough job. But I don't believe you can do the Washington job thoroughly with a group.

In reply to the direct question "Are you satisfied that these organizations are speaking for the general business community?" two participants said:

> They reputedly are, but I don't think they necessarily represent the views of the business community.

* * *

> I can say that we do not feel that they consistently represent us.

Several of these criticisms were brought into sharper focus by one participant who was interested essentially in legislative matters.

. . . they are not of any value to me at all (in working on legislation) because of the difficulty they have in arriving at a position. They are all over the lot.

Yet despite these criticisms it is doubtful that any of the representatives would have urged his company to discontinue membership in these organizations. They are not ideal, but they are useful as a backstop and as a source of information, both general and specific. In this regard, they may be considered as supplementing the work of the company representative who has broad responsibilities. For those representatives who have little responsibility in the executive policy or legislative areas, these general groups provide a substitute, albeit a relatively poor one, for such activity.

Specialized Groups

Many of the round-table representatives were active members of what might be described as specialized groups. These groups cut across industry lines, yet the focus of their interest is considerably narrower than that of general purpose groups. There are, of course, varying degrees of specialization. One group, for example, is composed primarily of firms who do business with one of the armed services; another includes most defense contractors.

There was some discussion at the meeting whether service-linked groups should be considered specialized groups. For the most part, it seemed to be the view of the round-table participants that the primary purpose of these groups is to provide support for the services. Although it might be expedient for companies to belong to, and financially support, such groups, they were thought to be of little use to the representatives of their companies, except possibly for social or sales contacts.

There was some disagreement among the representatives as to whether the advantages of the specialized groups ran toward the government or toward their members. In support of the contention that these groups were primarily a service to some part of the government, one representative said:

I think these organizations are primarily a service to government rather than a service to industry. The only thing I can see is that you go and you have a chance to meet people with the same kind of interests that you have; you meet people who are in the key spots in government. Some day you might have some occasion to go to see one of these men that you met, and you are on a little bit better basis than if you hadn't seen him before. But I think it is more for their benefit than for industry. You can't justify them in terms of what industry gets out of them.

But there were numerous dissents among the representatives. One of them went on to describe the type of tangible benefit which his company got out of one of these groups.

The group sponsored a trip to one of the military installations. Our man went along; they had a fine day, an outing with the commanding officer down there. Within three weeks, we had a problem having to do with that installation, and our man went back to the commanding officer. He was happy to see us, and every door in the whole installation has been open ever since.

Another described the benefits of association-sponsored inspection trips in somewhat different terms:

They have all these laboratories trimmed up, and they have all of the staff there to tell what they are doing and what their programs are, and in the course of a day you get a good briefing on what this installation is doing.

If you were to try to go around on your own and pick this information up in the course of the day, you just couldn't get the kind of show that these fellows put on for one of these associations. I think it is a good way for you or one of your men to get an insight as to what goes on at Wright-Patterson field, or the arsenals and similar places; you get a good briefing in the course of one day.

But the activities of these specialized associations are by no means confined to visits, briefings, and socializing. One group, for example, has a series of working committees that deal with a broad spectrum of problems in the area of government-contractor relations, including such things as revisions in the Armed Services Procurement Regulations. On some problems, it works with other interested groups; on others, it works largely alone. There is no doubt that this type of activity is of help to the government in providing a convenient way of obtaining coordinated industry views. At the same time, it is equally of help to industry by providing a forum in which their ideas on such things as government regulations can be effectively channelled to government officials.

Trade Associations

The companies of every representative at the conference belong to at least one trade association. Most belong to several, as either principal or associate members. One company represented belongs to some seventy-five since it is a major supplier of products to a broad spectrum of industry. But there is usually one trade association with which the representative keeps in contact and which represents his company's main trade interests. The closeness of these contacts appeared to vary widely depending on the association and the particular role of the company in the industry.

The feeling was expressed that for large companies, with manifold governmental interests, trade association representation cannot provide an adequate substitute for a Washington company representative. Good company representation in Washington, it was felt, tends to supplant many trade association activities and can be focused more specifically on the interests of the company. Reliance on trade associations is perhaps satisfactory for small companies that do not have Washington representatives; but for large ones it is not enough.

In part, the feeling that trade associations lack effectiveness for the larger companies stems from the fact that they are often characterized by a lack of cohesion or unity of purpose. One participant feels that:

> It is too complicated for large businesses to get together in a trade association on many issues because of inevitable differences in their interests and objectives. Look at the reciprocal trade issue, for example.

Still another criticism of trade association effectiveness that was mentioned is a lack of aggressiveness on their part in securing favorable decisions by the government. One of the representatives expressed the problem as follows:

> The interesting thing to me is that a lot of these associations don't do the kind of things that you would expect them to do.
> Now, I found during the Korean War that I could get decisions

that affected not only my company, but every other company in the industry. Why some of these associations don't do some of the obvious things is hard to explain, but I think it is a characteristic of the management of the associations. If you have a good, well-organized association, they really do a job. If you haven't, they don't.

In brief, the consensus of the round table seemed to be that for large companies it is not sufficient to rely on trade association representation. The better associations that are active on the Washington level are sometimes a useful adjunct to the work of the representative, but they are hardly a substitute for it.

Other Groups

Several members of the round table mentioned other types of groups, some formal, some informal, with which they have contact. Among these are several informal luncheon and discussion groups, various *ad hoc* groups organized under government auspices, scientific and professional groups, and the like.

Reference has already been made to the weekly construction luncheon groups, which form a kind of information exchange and meeting ground for representatives and others with a special interest. The general organizations sponsor several other such groups; so do various trade associations. And there are several informal groups, not sponsored by any association, that have been meeting over a number of years for sociability and the exchange of information. Most of the round-table participants belong to at least one such luncheon and discussion group, and several belong to three or four.

The focus of the informal groups is varied. Some are product-, industry-, or material-oriented. Some are functionally-oriented, as for example, labor relations. A luncheon speaker, usually from government, who gives an off-the-record talk seems to be the main feature.

> We try to get someone who has something to say on a situation that is more or less current. That is all it is. It is strictly informative. It isn't for competitive advantage.
> We have no reporter; we close the doors, and we talk. We have had people from labor, a Cabinet member, a White House official; we have had every type you can think of.

In most of the groups the formal remarks are followed by a question period.

> In this setting, where it is a little like a press interview, pretty blunt questions are all right. In another setting—if you were calling on him in his office, for example—you wouldn't ask him some of these questions.

Another sort of group mentioned by several representatives is an *ad hoc* group recruited under government auspices to deal with a special problem, such as standardizing specifications for a broad band of materials. In the normal course of events, such matters might be handled through a trade association. But where several commodities or associations are involved, especially where there are difficult competitive problems, the government may recruit its own group.

> Let's say you want to talk about something like standardization of the thermal factors in roof insulation, and this brings in cork people, glass people, asbestos people, aluminum—you have a lot of different interests here who are vying in the marketplace; they can't get together in a closed room and try to do anything about it officially, so the logical thing to do is to use some department of government.
> There is no trade association that can pick this one up effectively, but the government can, and if we don't use these services we are missing a good 'bet.

Several of the representatives have occasion to maintain contact with one or more of the professional or scientific societies.

> The scientific organizations can be very helpful in government activities. Many times the government relies upon them to set up certain groups to help in deliberations on very technical subjects where they believe those organizations are better qualified to handle it than an ordinary trade association.
> At least in my particular field, I rely a lot on those technical and professional organizations in dealing with the government.

All of these various groups: general and special purpose, trade associations, informal, *ad hoc*, and scientific groups, are at once a resource, a problem, and a challenge to the representative. They are a resource to the extent that they are sources of information and can be relied upon to follow, and perhaps act on, matters that are beyond the responsibility or the resources of the representative. They are a problem in the sense that they are so numerous as to constitute a considerable liaison task, and yet, because of the nature of their membership, they are rendered ineffective in many controversial matters. They are a challenge in the sense that the representative must do a job of representing his company to the government which is substantially superior to any one or combination of associations. This, of course, applies primarily to those representatives who have major nonmarketing responsibilities.

In general the representatives appear to accept the various groups and associations as part of the Washington environment. They are critical of several aspects of the job that some of the groups do, especially in their role as spokesmen for business. At the same time it is clear that the representatives have learned to make effective use of the resources of the groups and associations when they can be of help.

RELATIONS WITH WASHINGTON SPECIALISTS

In addition to groups and associations with which the representative has considerable dealings, the private specialist is also in the Washington picture. The most common type of specialist is the lawyer, with public relations specialists running a poor second numerically. At one of the round tables some attention was given to the question of what liaison there is between the representatives and these, or other, specialists.

Lawyers

In the first instance, it should be noted that a considerable number of company representatives are themselves lawyers and that a still larger number of practicing attorneys serve as company representatives. As one participant described it:

> I think there are probably more lawyers in town who act as representatives of companies across the board than there are representatives like the people around this table.
> In fact, a very substantial part of the law practice in Washington is really representation of a company and its sales, as well as a lot of strictly legal matters. They operate in sales, not by going out and peddling the products themselves, but through their contacts, setting up meetings for the sales managers of companies whom they repre-

sent and doing a certain amount of entertaining and things of that kind.

The legal specialists referred to in this section are essentially lawyers, *qua* lawyers, while the participating representatives who happen to be lawyers do not regard themselves as legal specialists.

For the most part, the companies represented at the round table have some kind of legal counsel in Washington. A few have resident house counsel, perhaps with a considerable staff. These house counsels specialize in particular areas: patents, taxes, or practice before a regulatory body. The majority of the companies, however, have continuing relations with a Washington law firm (or two), sometimes on a retainer basis and sometimes on a continuing, but case-to-case, basis.

One participant who represents several small companies indicated that legal representation is by no means the exclusive province of the large company.

> I would say that any company that does any volume of business at all with the government has a Washington counsel—either someone they call on occasionally or someone they retain full time. Even the small companies I represent hire legal counsel from time to time. I handle a lot of things for them, but when it comes to actual legal advice, they get legal counsel.

For the most part, the work of Washington counsel (either house or independent) is directed from headquarters and is not the responsibility of the representative, although this does not mean that there is not close liaison between the representative and counsel. An exception to this generality is the field of legislation in those cases where the representative has considerable direct legislative responsibility. In such instances the legal specialist, particularly if he engages in "lobbying," is subject to the immediate control of the representative, although the substance of his testimony or line of argument is probably worked out at headquarters.

It appeared that most of the companies use their legal counsel to provide legislative representation if the Washington representative does not perform this function. Thus a tax lawyer or an antitrust lawyer often does any lobbying or testifying that is to be done on a piece of technical legislation in these fields.

Several of the representatives expressed some doubt as to the effectiveness of lawyers in dealing with government except in actual litigation. For example:

> When you go into many places around Washington with a problem, if you take a lawyer with you or if you identify yourself as a lawyer, they wonder what is up that you need a lawyer on this particular problem; you may be a lot better off if you keep the lawyers out of it when you can.

Another said:

> They will say, "This fellow has troubles. He is bringing his lawyer with him."

A third representative pointed out:

> We have lots of negotiations with all kinds of government agencies —particularly contract negotiations. When you first enter into it, it is all right to bring a contract man, but don't bring a lawyer. If you bring a lawyer there, he will find more faults than the legal counsel of the Department of Defense will.

On the other hand, when asked whether they regard Washington counsel (house or independent) as competitive, or potentially competitive, with their own activities, the representatives were unanimous in their feeling that this is not really a problem. To the contrary, one representative said that he believed that a Washington counsel (or other specialist) is a valuable supplement to his own work.

> I think there is another thing that happens with these specialists. After you use a specialist or have him on a retainer, he may be in a better position to see where he can be of service to you. Of course, he has a commodity to sell. If he thinks he can be of service, he is not too reticent about saying, "Here is a place where I think I could be useful."
>
> Where this is the case, you know from the interest that is indicated —from their alertness—that there is a continuity of interest, and they do keep watching out for ways in which they can be helpful to your company.

Public Relations Specialists

Several of the companies represented at the round-table conferences use Washington public relations specialists. Some are employees of the company; some are independent practitioners. The range of their activities is broad—from handling general publicity and press relations in Washington to handling legislation and providing legislative intelligence.

> We have a public relations firm in town here which is heavily in legislative intelligence, although none of their people is registered. Their principal reputation is in this area. It is an invaluable adjunct to my office. I call them in for special assignments.

In most cases, however, outside public relations counsel appears to be brought in on a less regular basis, as for example to handle press coverage at a large company exhibition or demonstration to military personnel. The few companies that maintain in-house public relations personnel in Washington appear to be those with either a large number of visits from top management or a considerable amount of Washington press work.

Other Specialists

Several of the representatives mentioned that their companies maintain various industry or functional specialists or consultants, either at headquarters or in Washington. For example, a company that does extensive business as both a supplier and a customer of the petroleum industry maintains a petroleum industry expert at its corporate headquarters. This expert is available to the representative as needed. And, of course, in such specialized functional areas as industrial relations, taxation, and the like, the representative can draw on what, in several companies, are substantial departments, just as in the case of R & D problems he draws on the scientists and technical people in the company's laboratories.

SUMMARY

In carrying out his various duties, the Washington representative has available to him, and must take into account, a large number of groups, associations, and specialists. Although it might be supposed that the activities of these groups, associations, and specialists would be regarded as competitive with the work of the representatives, this does not appear to be the case. Rather they are looked upon as a resource to be used where appropriate. There is some dissatisfaction with the effectiveness of the groups and associations both as spokesmen for business and in the legislative and executive field. The groups, especially the general purpose groups, are accused of being too big and over-extended. Most of the representatives feel that they are in a position to do a much more precisely focused job for their companies than any group or series of groups can. This is true both of representatives who have their main responsibilities in the marketing area and also of those who are more broadly oriented or are exclusively oriented to executive policy or legislative matters. Much the same attitudes seem to apply to specialists, although some doubts were expressed as to the usefulness of lawyers in what are essentially nonlegal roles.

8

The Company's View of Washington Representation

WHAT DO TOP BUSINESS executives expect of their Washington representatives? Are they concerned about the relations of the representatives with various levels of company personnel? How do they go about appraising the effectiveness of the job that is being done in Washington for their company? What changes have been made or are being considered in the functions of Washington representatives?

To explore these questions, thirteen company headquarters were visited during the last months of 1959 and the early months of 1960. Interviews were held with the company's chief executive officer or his deputy, or with the immediate "boss" of the Washington representative if he was not the chief executive officer.

These company interviews were open-ended in the sense that they were not based on a fixed questionnaire. In each interview an effort was made to raise the main points that had evolved from the round-table conferences and to cover any special factors affecting representation for the specific company involved. In addition, there was at least general discussion of the functions of the company's Washington office to determine significant changes that had taken place since the conferences or that were being considered. This chapter presents the main points developed in these company interviews, especially if they deviate either in direction or in emphasis from the conclusions suggested by the record of the conferences.

Of the companies interviewed, except for one that had materially altered and expanded the functions of its representative in the political and legislative area, no major functional shifts appear to have occurred in the eighteen months that elapsed between the conferences and the interviews. To the extent that changes had taken place in what the representatives do and what their companies want them to do, such changes were in emphasis rather than in primary direction.

In general it can be said that there is a high degree of consistency between the functional areas of activity that the representatives described as being included in their responsibilities and the areas in which their bosses want them to work and think that they are working. But while there are no discrepancies between the basic job of representation as described at the conferences and the job as viewed at the main office, there are, in some cases, differences of view as to the way in which these functions are carried out and as to the degree of operating responsibility and authority possessed by the representative.

With few exceptions, the company does not look on the representative as its "ambassador plenipotentiary" at the seat of government. He is regarded more as a specialized minister than as a representative with full decision-making or policy-establishing authority. In short, in the company interviews, there tended to be less underscoring of representation as a substantive operating activity and more emphasis on its facilitative staff aspects. The operating authority, according to the company executives interviewed, is retained primarily in headquarters, and the representative does not appear to be a full-fledged member of the home office policy-making group even though his advice is sought and he does contribute to policy decisions.

This difference is perhaps not surprising. It may help to explain some of the indefiniteness which certain of the representatives pointed out in connection with defining their jobs and working out their relations with their companies. But it raises a question whether it is realistic to assume that Washington representatives can do a complete job of representation unless they participate actively in policy formation and play a substantive operating role in the development and execution of a government relations program.

MARKETING

It will be recalled from previous chapters that in several instances the primary, if not the exclusive, function of the representative lies in the broad area of marketing. This does not mean necessarily that the representative is a "salesman" in the usual sense of the word. Rather it implies that he is concerned primarily with the disposal of the company's services or products, directly or indirectly, now or in the future.

In discussing these marketing functions with headquarters officials, the variety of roles played by Washington representatives described at the round table was brought into clearer focus. At one extreme was a company that stated that it is not eager to acquire extensive government contracts in peacetime in either the R & D or the production area. It does not want its representative to develop a large number of leads for immediate contracts since the company regards its commercial projects and products as more profitable and desirable. What it does want is someone in Washington who can keep open its channels to government so that, in the event of another emergency, it could immediately acquire government contracts that would take the place of lost commercial orders for its products.

At the other end of the spectrum is a company that is seriously concerned about its government contracts—both R & D and production—and is greatly strengthening its Washington office in order to acquire more such contracts. In between, there are other companies that have a major interest in the marketing function and are satisfied with their existing Washington offices.

At several of the company headquarters the growing intensity of competition for government contracts was clearly apparent. Certain of these companies already enjoy a considerable volume of government business, most of it in the defense or defense-related areas in both R & D and in production. In several other companies, government contracts currently account for a relatively small proportion of the company's sales, but there is a desire to increase government business appreciably. Two of the companies visited are actively engaged in a reappraisal of the ways in which they go about securing government business and are reconsidering how their Washington offices are organized and perform, although no personnel or organizational changes have as yet been made.

The approach to Washington representation in the marketing area tends to depend considerably upon the basic motives that the company has for seeking government work. As stated in the interviews, these motives run the gamut from a belief that the company can "contribute to the defense effort" to a belief that government contracts are essential to the future of the company since R & D is becoming so important to future industrial existence and so much of it is sponsored by the government. This feeling is often accompanied by the companion belief that there is little profit in government R & D work and that profits lie in production only. It is inevitable, therefore, that production contracts are also sought.

In fact there is some evidence that the whole interest in, and approach to, solicitation of government business may well be changing. The R & D function tends to absorb an increasingly large share of any particular project, and there is a decline in the number of items being developed that involve long production runs. In addition there appears to be growing competition among defense contractors for a shrinking number of projects as greater reliance is placed on large prime contractors. Although a number of companies expressed the view that their scientific personnel could be more profitably employed on commercial product development, there seemed to be at least some appreciation of the fact that defense work or other government work could furnish a base on which a considerably larger scientific and technical effort could be built.

In both of the companies that were actively planning to launch major assaults on the government contract market, it was clearly indicated that the Washington representative was in no way responsible for the fact that the company had heretofore had little government business. Officials recognized that it was primarily a reflection of company policy, and no blame was placed on the Washington office. Indeed, in these two companies the attitude seemed to be that the representative had perhaps tended to be a little impatient with the company because of its previous failure to adopt policies and plans that would attract more government contracts. He was regarded as a "voice crying in the wilderness" that had only recently been heard by top management. In neither of these companies was there any indication that under the changed marketing policy the Washington office would be called upon to behave any differently than it had in the past, or that it would have to be appreciably increased in size.

Another company that has substantial defense work took a considerably less aggressive point of view toward its Washington marketing activities. This company wants government work but is not dependent upon it and, to the extent that it takes on government contracts, it wants them to fit into the general area of its commercial products. It believes that its government business will stem primarily from the contacts that its top executives and its key scientific and technical people have with the services and that its Washington office is essentially facilitative. It relies upon this office to keep it informed, to "make the rounds," to put out small fires when they arise. But it is clear that it does not hold the Washington office responsible for the conduct of its marketing program in the government contract field since its executives and scientific and technical personnel are almost constantly in Washington or at government laboratories and centers elsewhere.

One company, which also has a considerable volume of government work, has evolved, since the time of the round-table conferences, a fairly elaborate structure for handling it. It has recently established a division to develop, manufacture, and market defense products. The Washington representative serves not only this division but also other divisions of the company that might sell the company's nondefense products to the government. But defense products account for a large fraction of the company's government sales, and the division has a considerable marketing staff of its own. In addition, the functional marketing staff at company headquarters is available to help in the sale of the company's products and services to the government, as is a special government relations staff. In this structure it is difficult to determine just where the Washington representative (who has no legislative or nonmarketing executive agency responsibilities) fits.

Reference was made in Chapter 3 to the fact that several companies maintain extensive establishments in Washington, not to secure government contracts, but rather to maintain liaison with government agencies, especially in the R & D area. The focus is on learning about new scientific or technical advances or on discovering new product requirements. In the latter case some companies prefer to develop at their own expense a product that meets the requirement and sell it "off-the-shelf" to the government.

To these functions must be added the function of the "standby" office. As already indicated, one company stated that it does not wish to take on any further government contracts now but does want to keep itself in a position to acquire contracts quickly in the event that another emergency should cut off its main civilian markets. Clearly it has in mind another emergency like the Korean War, when its civilian markets might be drastically curtailed owing to priorities, controlled materials, and the like.

The next few years are likely to place a considerable strain on existing Washington office functions and personnel of companies that do, or want to do, a considerable volume of direct business with the government, especially in the defense area. Some companies may resolve this by "beefing up" their present offices. Others may meet the problem by having units or offices from headquarters handle their governmental marketing, either by moving them to Washington or by having their officials visit Washington frequently. But as competition increases for the contract dollar, the marketing efforts of those who want such contracts seem destined to become more intensive and more sophisticated.

Just what the role of a Washington office will be in this intensified marketing effort is hard to foretell. If the headquarters is far removed from Washington, it seems probable that the Washington representative will take on additional importance and stature in this effort and may be assigned more substantive operating responsibility. This seems, for example, to be the typical position of the Washington offices of west coast aircraft companies, where distance and the importance of the government as a customer dictate a sizable and strong office. For companies whose headquarters are nearer at hand and which are not so extensively dependent on the government, major government marketing responsibility will probably remain in headquarters, with the Washington office playing essentially a facilitative staff role.

NONMARKETING EXECUTIVE AGENCY ACTIVITY

One conclusion that can be drawn from the round-table conferences (Chapter 4) is that national companies do not make any appreciable effort to influence administration policy in the executive agencies through their Washington representatives. This conclusion was generally confirmed by the company interviews. To the extent that companies expressed themselves on questions of administration policy, it was indicated that this function is usually reserved for headquarters personnel.

In this connection again the Washington representative plays essentially a facilitative staff role in the sense that he participates, advises, and assists, but is not expected alone to handle policy negotiations regularly or take a position. This does not mean, of course, that the Washington representative is supposed to stay away from the executive agencies. In many cases his company expects that he will be a frequent visitor there, but the purpose of his calls is to maintain contacts, if possible, to discover what is going on, and to handle administrative problems that may arise between the company and the department.

An exception to this general rule is the case of regulated companies, where the representative is expected not only to perform the essentially administrative liaison functions but also to engage in policy matters as well, calling upon headquarters personnel for guidance as needed. This situation is parallel to that found in the marketing area. Companies heavily involved in defense work tend to have larger Washington offices with considerable operating authority. The regulatory body can, in its own way, have an impact on a regulated company similar to that of the Department of Defense or a military service on a missile manufacturer. Hence regulated companies have tended to clothe their Washington offices with a somewhat greater degree of substantive responsibility than do nonregulated companies that are not heavily dependent on government contracts.

In only one instance of nonregulated, nondefense companies was there any indication that the company assigned its Washington representative substantive operating authority in dealing with executive agencies. It is perhaps significant that this company is in an industry that is threatened with partial regulation of certain of its activities. In the other companies there appeared to be little appreciation of the relationship between the status and function of the Washington office and the impact of governmental policy as developed in the executive branch—even on a large company, not regulated or heavily dependent on government business. There was a good deal of complaint voiced about many administration policies, but this is not an area where the Washington representative is held responsible for doing much beyond making contacts on an *ad hoc* basis.

As was seen in Chapter 4, the executive branch contacts of the representatives, apart from the marketing area, are numerous, and they are expected to be so. But the general view in headquarters is that these contacts are essentially facilitative in nature.

ACTIVITIES ON THE HILL

It will be recalled from Chapter 5 that only one of the representatives at the round-table conferences has primary responsibility for legislative activities. As his functions were realigned shortly before the conferences, he devotes himself almost exclusively to legislation of concern to his company. Two or three of the other representatives do considerable legislative work although this is certainly not their exclusive function. Some other representatives indicated that they get involved in activities on the Hill on only a sporadic basis.

Following the end of the conferences, one of the representatives, whose functions theretofore had not been precisely defined, was assigned to legislative work as a primary responsibility. As indicated elsewhere, this new assignment appears to have been stimulated in part by the representative himself. The company has few direct dealings with the government and is not regulated. It does have, however, serious labor, tax, and depreciation problems and is subject to considerable competitive pressure. The assignment of its representative to legislative work is part of an over-all company program to strengthen its position in the political area generally. As a part of this program the company expects its representative to get acquainted with the senators and representatives from states and districts in which it has plants, to "educate" them on the consequences of proposed legislation, to follow closely legislation of interest and concern to the company, and to keep headquarters up to date on its progress. Since the program began, this representative has devoted a major share of his time, according to headquarters personnel, to legislative work. Headquarters personnel believe that the program is useful and that regular contacts with members of Congress will prove valuable.

In contrast, no particular stress is laid on legislative activity by the majority of the company interviewees. Beyond knowing at least the key senators and representatives from "home" states and districts and having the ability to move around the Hill, headquarters does not appear to expect any appreciable amount of legislative activity on the part of its representatives. This in general jibes with the conclusions of the round-table conferences that the Hill is not a major area of activity for most representatives.

BUSINESS AND POLITICS

It will be recalled that at several sessions of the round table considerable attention was paid to the role of "business and politics" in shaping the responsibilities of the representative. Judging from the comments of the headquarters personnel, a majority of the companies interviewed now have active "business and politics" programs in operation or are in the process of working up programs in this field.

There was a certain amount of reluctance on the part of headquarters personnel to discuss company programs in this area. But there was little question that it is an area that was receiving considerably more attention than it did two years earlier. As a minimum, in the programs that have evolved, or are evolving, top management, as a matter of policy, encourages company personnel to take an active interest and participate in politics, regardless of party. A few companies have confined such encouragement essentially to supervisory personnel. Several have designated someone in the headquarters staff to be responsible for implementation of the policy at field levels.

A few firms indicated that they have gone a step further and have set up mechanisms for transmitting company views and positions on various issues to company employees. One firm indicated that it plans to give such views to active politicians, and two other companies indicated that they already do so on a limited basis. None of the companies indicated that it has entered, or intends to enter, the field of political action—i.e. to support or attempt to defeat politicians who are friendly or hostile to what the company management regards as the company's interests. The theory seems to be that by activating company personnel politically and advising them of the company's interests in specific areas, the company point of view will be forcefully transmitted to politicians without any direct company action.

The role that a Washington representative plays, or is supposed to play, in such programs was not precisely defined. In the case of one company, the program clearly has in part to be stimulated by the representative. But in other cases, the view was expressed that it is undesirable to use the representative except in a most general way in conjunction with these programs. He is supposed to follow legislation of interest to the company. He is supposed to make contacts on the Hill or arrange contacts for others for the purpose of explaining company positions. But typically it is contemplated that he will have relatively little responsibility for the "business and politics" program, and in several instances he has not even been consulted on it.

It should be pointed out that, in most cases, the political programs for those companies that have them have not yet fully evolved and are still being worked on in headquarters. But the view was expressed at several companies that the representative would tend to lose his usefulness if he became identified with any program that went beyond simply passing the word to supervisors or employees that the company was anxious to have them engage in political activity, as individuals, in the party of their choice. In such limited programs there is little that the representative could, in fact, do. It must also be remembered that few of the representatives have any direct responsibility for legislation, and few have major roles to play in influencing, or trying to influence, administration policy in the executive agencies.

ORGANIZATIONS

Most of the interviewees were asked to what extent the various general business organizations and trade associations can be relied upon to give them adequate, if indirect, representation in Washington. The reaction of most of those interviewed, just as of the representatives, to questions about the general business organizations was by and large negative. The general organizations are typically viewed as not being effective and not always expressing the views of the management. On the other hand, several of those interviewed said that the job being done by such organizations is being improved.

Reaction to the adequacy of trade associations was more mixed. In some instances the replies were favorable; in others largely negative. But by and large the headquarters executives agreed with their representatives that wholly adequate representation cannot be secured through reliance on either general business organizations or trade associations.

In part the usefulness of business organizations and trade associations, as seen by a number of company executives, is related to the fact that they do not wish their companies to become too prominent on the Washington scene. This is one of the reasons why these companies have no intention of increasing the size of their Washington operations and also why they tend to continue to rely upon organizations and associations for partial representation on many industry-wide issues. This attitude appears to be rooted in the idea that "out of sight is out of mind" and that if a company becomes too active in Washington, it may draw the attention of demagogues or "professional" investigators.

RELATIONS WITH THE COMPANY

It will be recalled that at the round-table conferences several of the representatives expressed some concern about the lack of clear-cut organizational lines within which they could operate. The typical pattern is for the representative to report to the company through an executive in the sales department—perhaps the vice-president for sales or the vice-president for government sales. To the extent that the representative spends a considerable portion of his time and effort on nonmarketing activities and that these activities are growing in importance to the success of his company, he believes that this organizational pattern tends to weaken his position somewhat and that it would be better if he reported higher up in the company, to either the president or the executive vice-president. Those representatives at the round-table conferences who do so report indicated that they believe that it helps them in carrying out their responsibilities.

Virtually no concern was expressed in the headquarters interviews about the representative's relations with his company. It was generally agreed in those interviews that the channels through which the representative reports are vague. It was conceded that the representative does, and indeed is expected to, go "out of channels" frequently. But the concern that a number of representatives have expressed about these informal and sometimes vague channels is not shared by their principals at headquarters. None of those interviewed who are the immediate superiors of the representatives indicated that a change in the existing channel of reporting is essential. Nor did those who are concerned primarily with marketing activities give any indication that they are impatient with the amount of time that the representatives have to give to nonmarketing activities. They want to be kept generally informed of these activities, but on an after-the-fact basis. In short, the principals seemed to be quite satisfied with the existing channels by which the representatives report, both formal and informal.

The executives interviewed at headquarters agreed with the views expressed by the representatives that an important aspect of representation is an intimate knowledge of the company, its products or services, and its personnel. The executives acknowledged that in most cases such knowledge can probably best be acquired by spending considerable time in the company in a variety of jobs. Hence they believe that in choosing a successor to the present representative, they would probably pick a company man in preference to someone who knows his way around Washington but who has never worked at the company. This view applies particularly with respect to representatives who have extensive marketing responsibility for a large and technical product line. On the other hand, the principals also lay heavy stress on the ability of the representative to get around Washington and to make a large number and wide variety of contacts in different departments and offices and at different echelons.

Without exception, the company interviewees expressed the opinion that their present representatives are doing a highly satisfactory job, essentially along the lines that were expected, but that the duties and responsibilities of the representatives are so broad and varied that it is virtually impossible to have either a single yardstick or a series of yardsticks for measuring performance. This is true even in the marketing area. In the field of legislative and executive agency contacts, the work of the representatives is still more intangible. Assessment of whether the representatives are performing the job that their companies want them to perform has to be left largely to the judgment of the company executives to whom the representatives report or with whom they came in frequent contact. Despite the seeming vagueness of these standards of performance, several company executives said they believe that they can tell with tolerable accuracy whether a representative is performing effectively.

SUMMARY

There are no striking differences between the job as described at the round-table conferences and as described by executives interviewed at company headquarters. Yet there was some distinction in focus and emphasis. In the company interviews more stress was put on the facilitative "staff" elements of the job—advising, assisting, maintaining contacts, finding out and reporting on what is going on in the government, and expediting administrative action. At the same time company executives placed less emphasis on (or showed less recognition of) the substantive operating role of representation, that is, responsibility for the development of a marketing program and the generation of sales volume, active participation in the establishment of company policy on legislation or administration policy, decision-making in negotiations on major substantive matters with executive branch officials, and the like. Stated another way, while the representatives would prefer to function as ambassadors with substantial powers and may regard their jobs in this way, their superiors, for the most part, look upon the representative's job as coming a bit farther down the diplomatic scale.

This difference in emphasis is not surprising. If anything, future developments may well bring about a reorientation of the job of representation so that it is much closer in reality to the job as seen by the representatives than by the company executives. It must be recalled that the sample of company interviews is small. It was not possible to conduct an interview at the headquarters of one company represented at the round tables whose Washington office is more broadly conceived and based than that of most of those participating in the seminars. As companies gradually develop more sharply defined policies with respect to their relations with the government—whether marketing, legislative, or administration policy—it seems probable that they will tend to change their "legations" into "embassies."

9

The Future of Washington Representation

Regardless of defense budgets, regardless of government budgets in general, the importance to industry of Washington, and hence Washington representation, is going to be even greater in the future than it is today. . . .

* * *

I think there will be far more companies represented in Washington because competition will become keener and Washington will become the hub for most industry.

For that reason, I think that not only will more companies have representatives in Washington, but their offices are going to become larger and more extensive and will undertake a wider range of activities.

REGARDLESS OF THE SPAN of their present activities, the Washington representatives at the round-table conferences believe that the functions of representation will continue to expand. Most of the representatives also feel that more large companies will be represented in Washington in the future. There is less unanimity about the future representation of small business—either directly or indirectly through trade associations and business groups.

Several participants prefaced their comments by saying that the nature of governmental activity over the next decade will largely shape the nature of business representation. Given a continuation of large government expenditures for defense and other purposes and a growth in the degree of control that the government exercises over the economy as a whole, these representatives agree that expanded representation is inevitable. But they indicated that shifts in existing trends

114

in government could sharply alter trends in the nature and level of representation. Still others tended to equate the future expansion of functions of Washington representation with the relative strength of management and labor. Constantly growing labor power, they believe, would call out increased attempts by business firms to balance such power.

LEGISLATION AND POLITICAL ACTION

Almost all participants expect the legislative activities of Washington representatives to increase over the next decade. This feeling is shared by those who presently do and those who do not work in the legislative field. Two quite different views, however, were taken of this predicted increase in legislative activity. One group tended to view it as essentially technical legislative work on a nonpartisan, nonpolitical basis, largely isolated from anything their companies might do locally. Others see it as part and parcel of increased political action by businesses and businessmen. This does not mean that the representatives will work, or direct work, at the grass-roots political level for the company. Rather, they will work with elected representatives, whose election was, hopefully, favorably influenced by company action in the field. One representative of a large company described the plans of his company as follows:

> So that gives us—to use sales terminology—about seventy-five sales contacts on the Hill that we feel we can go to because we make a major contribution to the economic well-being of their districts.
> We are not covering those contacts right now. Anyone in sales knows that one salesman can't cover seventy-five customers well, especially the contacts I am talking about. I hope we can add one man so we can do it a little better and, through home-town contacts, develop a double-barreled attack so that not only can I call on legislators here, but we can get our people back home to talk the same language.
> In addition to the importance of direct contact from the grass roots, if you get your plant man out in the field interested in a subject, he will talk about it in his area, at the Chamber of Commerce, the Rotary and Kiwanis Clubs, and so forth.

This same representative went on to emphasize the need to keep the Washington representative out of direct political and partisan involvement at the grass-roots level:

> Directing partisan, grass-roots efforts out of Washington is a major mistake because you immediately get a partisan label, which can handicap a good Washington representative. That doesn't mean that we as Washington representatives don't have an interest at the local level. We do, but my recommendation is that any activity in the political area, up to and including election day, should be directed out of headquarters. We don't want to set ourselves up as partisan politicians down here.

The feasibility of this dichotomy between partisan activity at the local level and a nonpartisan, nonpolitical stance in Washington was questioned by some representatives. One, whose company operates in a particularly sensitive political environment, said that if his company were engaged in grass-roots political activity, even if it were not party-oriented, his job in Washington would become much more difficult, if not impossible, because he would inevitably be viewed as a partisan.

Another put the difficulty of separating local and Washington political activity in the following terms:

> In other words, you say you are supposed to work at the local level, and I agree. You work with this man, or you try to, and you find out he is not dependable. What is the word going to be back at the home office? Can you say "Tell the people to go out and try to defeat that man. He is no good for us."

It became apparent that the future functions of the representatives would be strongly affected by the kind and degree of local political activity in which their companies engaged. If the company was inactive or largely inactive, the representative could probably continue to represent it, in either the executive or the legislative branch, on a wholly nonpartisan basis.[1] If, on the other hand, the company became closely identified with the interests of a particular party, then it seemed likely that the representative would tend to be more effective with an

---

[1] While the great majority of the representatives individually appeared from their comments to be Republicans and although they may have felt more comfortable during the Eisenhower Administration, there was no evidence that they were ineffective during the Truman and Roosevelt Administrations.

administration and legislators of that party and less effective with administrations and legislators of the other party. A third possibility is that the company would become politically active but would not become affiliated, or closely identified, with either one of the major political parties. In the latter situation the company could adopt either of two courses. It could become active only in the event that a representative of either party from a district or state in which it was interested was consistently hostile or uncooperative, or alternatively, it could be continuously active in both parties (in two-party districts or states) in the selection of candidates.

Whether active or quiescent politically, the representatives clearly expected that they would find themselves working increasingly "up on the Hill," and they believed that their company managements would take more interest in national legislation. This does not mean that every large company would have an extensive legislative program covering all aspects of social, international, and economic legislation. Rather the trend was regarded as being toward a more modest effort, with the company taking an interest in legislation of specific concern to it and in a small number of bills of broad economic interest. The Chamber of Commerce, the National Association of Manufacturers, other general business groups, and the multiplicity of trade associations would continue to be the primary legislative spokesmen for business. But they would be more directly and actively supported by individual companies.

The representatives were asked whether they themselves feel a responsibility for arousing a greater measure of political and/or legislative awareness among the representatives of management of their companies. One of them replied:

> We have a function of trying to sell top management on the fact that something should be done in this area; but I don't think Washington representatives should direct such an activity or have too much to do with the actual running of a program for the purpose.

This led naturally to the question whether the company's political views essentially reflected the long-run economic interests of the company or simply the political preferences and prejudices of the current top management. Two opposing views were expressed:

I think that when a Washington representative, or any other representative, of a corporation comes down here and expounds on a political issue, he is really speaking for the head man of his company and should reflect that man's views—not those of the stockholders or a possible successor.

and:

I don't think a personal, individual view is important. It is the effect of that legislation on the company that counts, and that isn't essentially personal opinion. You must look at what the legislation is going to do to you. Is it going to increase your costs, is it going to squeeze you out of certain markets? That does not depend on a personal political opinion; it is just economic good sense.

The question was asked whether company personnel who "buttonhole" senators or congressmen, especially at the local level, are speaking for themselves or as official company spokesmen. One participant pointed out that, both locally and in Washington, the approach is made in terms of the state or district.

"Senator So and So, there is a piece of legislation coming up that is going to influence the widget business in your state. We feel it is going to be detrimental to the economy of your state, and we thought you would like to know why."

If he is a congressman, "This bill, if it is passed, may affect the jobs of 1,200 employees in your district."

We try to pull it right down to the district, and we think if we do that, we make him stand still and listen, whether he is a Republican or a Democrat.

But regardless of the political program of the company, it was apparent that the primary focus of the representative in Washington who handles legislation would continue to be the same as it is now.

Our job is to work with elected officials after they are elected, and I don't care whether they are Democrats or Republicans or Progressives. If they represent the districts in which we have operations, it is our duty to work with them.

It seems probable that more representatives will have this type of responsibility in the years to come. They may be called in increasingly to advise their managements on national politics, but their main tasks will be to deal with "all comers" at the Washington level.

The advent of increased legislative and political responsibility for representatives might well come about quickly. As one representative said:

> I can see right now, just in the last six months here in Washington, a major trend in the direction of business getting into politics. In the last six weeks we have had people from four different companies come to us and ask what we do in the political arena because their top management wanted to do something. This is a growing movement, and I am pleased to see it because I think it is a necessary thing.

OTHER EXPANDING SUBSTANTIVE AREAS

Several other expanding substantive areas were mentioned. One of these is the international field, in which several representatives have a growing interest. In part this interest concerns the increased foreign sales that their companies are making—direct to consumers, through subsidiaries, or to foreign governments; greater emphasis on covering the foreign embassy "beat" as a means for soliciting export business is an illustration. In part, interest in international affairs is defensive, aimed at combating an increase in imports from foreign countries that compete with the company's products in domestic markets.

Another area that seems likely to demand an increased amount of attention from Washington representatives might be generally described as "R & D." As discussed in Chapter 2, research and development contracts, or at least information on government research and development, is of prime importance to several of the companies represented at the round-table conferences.

> Our emphasis has been more on the scientific side than ever before. The reason is simply that fifteen years ago the government spent about $100 million for research and development, and today it spends over $3 billion. The amount is going up all the time, and that is why we have increased our emphasis.

This representative believes that the upward trend in government research and development expenditures will continue and that his office will have to be set up to keep pace with such developments. This is in spite of the fact that his company does not have a large number of R & D contracts itself. Rather it feels obliged to follow scientific developments closely.

In view of this trend this representative was asked, "If you went out and got hit by a truck, would they replace you with a scientist?" He replied:

> I suppose they might, but I don't think so because they need someone who is a little broader and who will not be unhappy if he is forced to cover some problems quite superficially.
>
> You need to have a wide range of interests in your company affairs; you probably need considerable knowledge of all the aspects of your company's business, good judgment, and some aggressiveness.
>
> A scientist's training, on the other hand, is different from ours. He may want to go deeper into a problem than we can and cover a narrower range of problems.
>
> There is a limit to how much time a Washington man can spend on any one problem. He can't go too deeply and still cover them all.

Although the representatives indicated that the next ten years will see most Washington offices expand their functions, particularly in the areas set forth above, this does not mean that other existing functions will decrease in importance. On the contrary, the consensus was that coverage of the more traditional executive agency functions—marketing, information-gathering, and general liaison with the departments—will be intensified. Competition for government contracts is expected to be sharper so that not only will the Washington staffs have to be larger, but in some instances company field offices will have to be established or expanded for those items and systems the development or procurement of which takes place outside Washington.

THE STATUS OF THE REPRESENTATIVE

Several of the representatives said that the Washington representative of the future will have (and certainly should have) a more prominent role in the higher policy councils of his company. Some predicted this development would be a natural outgrowth of the trend toward a more active political and/or legislative role. Washington representation will gain in corporate stature primarily as a reflection of the increased importance of government "hardware" and research and development contracts to the company.

It was anticipated that increased stature for the representative would be reflected in several ways. One is that an increasing number of representatives would report to the company's chief executive officer or at least to an executive vice-president and fewer representatives would report through a functional headquarters officer, such as a vice-president for marketing or a vice-president for government products or a vice-president-general counsel; this shift in lines of reporting would reflect both increased stature and a broadened scope. Another expectation is that more Washington representatives would become officers of their companies, with vice-presidential rank. As indicated in Chapter 6, several members of the round table believe that such an upgrading would help them discharge their present duties. Increased rank would be a natural outgrowth of broadened and increased responsibilities.

One representative spoke specifically to the fact that the future strengthening of his office requires that he be made aware of the long-range plans and basic policies of his company at their inception.

> We do not get all of the reports from the basic policy-making and scientific committees that are of interest to us. We must know what the future plans and policies of the company are. Sometimes you are working in the dark, not knowing in what direction the company is going because you are not considered part of the group that gets these official reports. I think that holds true for a number of companies. It certainly holds true for ours.

SMALL BUSINESS REPRESENTATION

Since virtually all of the representatives at the conferences were employed by large national companies, it was perhaps natural that they doubted whether small companies could afford, or needed, to maintain representation. This thought was expressed as follows:

> I think the league here is too big for small companies. There is very little place for small companies except under special situations. To be sure, smart, forward-looking small companies will have representation here, but you are not going to have Washington overrun with representatives of small companies. It is not going to be a league in which they can play.

In fact, a considerable number of small, or at least medium-sized, companies now maintain some type of representation, through either lawyers or other agents who look after the interests of a multiple clientele. For the most part these companies appear to be those which do a considerable amount of government business or which have special regulatory problems. Other smaller firms tend to rely for broad industry or general representation on some combination of trade associations or general business groups, but some criticism of the effectiveness of this representation was expressed.

No solutions to this problem, however, were suggested by the group. Yet if large companies step up the scope of their representation, smaller firms almost inevitably will be forced to re-examine their own representation in those areas where their interests may diverge from those of larger companies. This is clear in the marketing area. It may be true in other fields as well.

VALIDITY OF THE FORECASTS

Before attempting to summarize the forecasts of the round-table participants, it is appropriate to comment briefly on the probable validity of these statements. It is a natural human tendency to attach importance to one's activities and to believe quite honestly that they will be of growing future importance. It is also easy, particularly in the Washington environment, to attach more significance than is warranted to short-term events and developments that may, at the time, appear to be of overriding importance.

On the other hand, events in general since the conferences seem to lend support to the belief that representation will be broadened and intensified. Undoubtedly a prime consideration in the forecasts of several of the participants was the political and governmental role of labor. Events since the spring of 1958—the elections of 1958, the passage of the Landrum-Griffin Act, the steel strike, the big city vote in the 1960 election—have underscored management-labor tensions, and announcements in the press and informal discussions clearly indicate the determination of a growing number of firms to take a more active part in governmental and political affairs to maintain a balance with labor's political strength. As this determination is translated into action, there is no doubt that it will generate a greater span of work and responsibility for the company's Washington representative in the legislative and perhaps the political areas.

Similarly in the fields of marketing and research and development, events since the conferences have lent support to the representatives' forecasts that they would have more to do in these areas than they have in the past. Growing competition, increasingly complex weapons and weapon systems, and new programs of scientific research all point to a probable step-up in these more traditional functional areas. Thus, while at first glance the representatives' forecasts of greater importance for their offices over the next decade might be discounted as wishful thinking, there are numerous indications to support their validity.

SUMMARY

An analysis of the trends forecast by the round-table group indicates what a typical or composite Washington representative of a national company in the late 1960's might be like and might do. The description will probably not fit any specific representative of any specific company but will indicate the range of his functions. Representatives of closely regulated industries may, of course, depart from the following pattern, as will representatives whose companies do not sell to the government.

In the first instance, the representative a decade hence will continue to discharge broad marketing functions. If anything, these will be intensified and will be more extensively manned by specialists. In the R & D field particularly there will be a strengthening, through the Washington office, of the liaison between the company's and the government's laboratories and scientific staffs. It is quite possible that the Washington office will have to be supplemented by field offices. Essentially the Washington office will serve as an embassy or key point of contact for the company in its relationship with the federal government. The representative will be charged with following and guiding, where possible, legislative and administrative actions and policies of both specific and general interest to the company. On matters of specific company interest he will be expected to take direct action. On matters of general interest he will be expected either to take direct action or else to coordinate the company's position and activity through trade and industry groups. The representative will be looked to as an important adviser on any company grass-roots campaign designed to improve the local, state, or national political climate. In general he will report to the top management of the company, more specifically, to that member of top management who is primarily responsible for the company's external relations.

In all probability the representative will have had broad experience in the company before coming to Washington and will have served an apprenticeship in Washington of up to five years before taking on primary responsibility for the Washington office. He will be an officer of the company. His professional background will be legal, scientific-engineering, or business administration, depending on the nature of the company's products. But more important than education and training will be his ability to command the respect and active support of a wide variety of company staff and operating officials and his ability to handle a multiplicity of problems affecting his company quickly and effectively.

It is probable that most large companies will have Washington offices and that many medium-sized or even smaller companies will also have offices if they do an appreciable volume of work for the government. The offices themselves will probably be larger than those of today, perhaps averaging ten people, not counting clerical personnel. Some of these people will work primarily on legislative matters.

The idea of increased and more effective representation for large companies will be viewed by some with mistrust. Admittedly these larger and more effective offices could have a considerable impact on government policies and actions that may not necessarily correspond with other views of "the public interest." On the other hand, there will be countervailing forces at work, and a considerable group of politicians and others will be vocally critical of irresponsible conduct. Furthermore, it is probably unrealistic and undesirable to hold that there should not be effective liaison and communication between government and major segments of the economy as represented by large companies. If the Washington offices are fully effective, they will not only transmit the views and desires of the company to government but will also serve as a conduit for information running from government to business. There is no doubt, however, that the Washington representative of the future, as his functions expand, will have to conduct his affairs with circumspection and on a high professional level.

Agenda for the Round-Table Conference of Washington Representatives

SESSION 1

Orientation

1. Opening remarks by Robert D. Calkins, President, The Brookings Institution, on the purposes, objectives, and methods of the conference.

2. Discussion of some of the basic concepts of Washington representation.
   a. What are the basic problems confronting companies which lead them to have Washington representatives?
   b. What contribution do Washington representatives make in solving these problems?
   c. What impact do they have on company policy? On the government?
   d. Is there any way of measuring the effectiveness of Washington representation?

3. Discussion of the range of activities in which Washington representatives engage.
   a. Checklist of activities.
   b. Activities not engaged in but which should be, in the opinion of the representatives.
   c. Are other functions performed by others? By whom?

4. Discussion of the coverage of the conference series and of the tentative agenda for the second session.

Relations with the Executive Branch

Discussion of the following functions, as they involve relations with executive agencies, in terms of the questions raised in the section below.

1. Secure research and development contracts and follow government activity in R & D.

2. Sell existing products to the government, either directly or indirectly as, for example, where actual procurement is handled outside of Washington.

3. Technical assistance to the government in connection with the company's products.

4. Assistance to customers in the handling of their government relations.

5. Information and data gathering and reporting and interchanging company information with government agencies.
   a. Scientific, technical, and R & D information.
   b. Statistical—general and pertaining to industry and company.
   c. General economic and political information.
   d. Service on advisory committees.

6. Defensive activity aimed at
   a. Furnishing government officials with the facts so that they will not, in ignorance, pursue a course of action which might be inimical to the interests of the company.
   b. Preventing competitive or opposing groups from getting favorable government action inimical to the interests of the company.

7. Positive action to advance a point of view.

8. Special problems involving regulatory agencies.

Questions concerning the above functional areas:

1. How are such functions carried out?
   a. In how many agencies?
   b. At what levels?
   c. By committee meetings, by visits to officials' offices, by phone, by entertainment? Other?
   d. How often?
   e. White House and party committee relations.
   f. Relations with regulatory bodies.

2. In conducting business with the executive agencies, does the Washington representative receive any help from others? What kind of help? How much?

    a. Others in own company.
    b. Trade association.
    c. Other groups or other representatives.
    d. Specialists—lawyers, lobbyists, public relations counsel, etc.
    e. Congressional.
    f. National or local political leaders.

3. What is the impact on the government of these dealings? How do government officials regard them?

    a. Do these relations tend to increase or decrease the cost of government?
    b. To what extent do they help the government official with his job—provide him with information, help him sell his program, etc.?
    c. To what extent are these activities viewed with suspicion?
    d. Is it possible to trace the effect of these relations on the policy or action of the government?

4. From the company's standpoint, how effective are these relations? How does, and how should, top management appraise the effectiveness of these relations?

    a. Are the demands made on Washington representatives in this area reasonable? Demand too much? Not enough?
    b. What standards for determining effectiveness of relations with executive agencies should management use?
    c. Is it possible to have a "profit and loss" statement for the Washington representative in this area?
    d. Aside from his own office, what are the main strengths and weaknesses that the participants have observed in the executive relations of other representatives?
    e. If the company's Washington office were closed, what would be the probable effect on the company over the next two years?

Relations with the Congress

1. Consideration of the following range of functions involving relations with the Congress:
   a. No direct contact but follow congressional activity, identifying and reporting on programs of general or specific interest to company.
   b. Maintain contact with members of Congress and congressional staff for information purposes only.
   c. Informal presentation of company views on both general and specific legislative programs to congressmen and staffs.
   d. Formal presentation of views.
   e. Handling of investigations aimed at company or industry.
   f. Participation in group efforts to secure passage or defeat of legislation in the face of opposition.
   g. Individual efforts to secure passage or defeat of legislation in the face of opposition.

2. Questions pertaining to the range of congressional relations:
   a. What and who determines the extent to which congressional relations are maintained, if at all? Should responsibility in this area be expanded? Why?
   b. What types of company problems call for congressional relations?
   c. How are such relations conducted?
   d. What sources of help are available to the representative in the conduct of these relations? To what extent does he work through others rather than directly?
   e. What is known about the reaction of congressmen and their staffs to these relations?
   f. How should the effectiveness of congressional relations be judged by top management? How is it judged?

Relations with the Company

1. To whom in the company does the representative report, formally and actually?

2. Who in the company carries the representative's budget? Why? Does this particular arrangement cause difficulty? Who promotes him—in fact and according to the manual?

3. What are the representative's relations with the chief executive officer of the company? Is the chief executive officer regarded as a "senior citizen" whose help and counsel is constantly sought on broad public questions? Does the chief executive officer use the representative effectively, both in his role as senior company executive and in his role as "senior citizen"? How could such use be made more effective? Are there any indications as to how the chief executive officer views the role and activities of the representative?

4. With what departments or divisions of the company does the representative have contact? With whom in these departments? On what types of problems? Are such contacts informal or formally provided for? How can the representative be helpful to these departments and divisions? Do they tend to make unreasonable demands on the representative? Do they fail to understand and use the services which he can provide for them?

5. How does the representative control and co-ordinate the Washington contacts of members of his company. Is such control and co-ordination important? Why?

6. What was the previous job experience of the representative? What was his educational background? Is there any pattern of educational or job experience that seems to be particularly helpful for the representative to have? Should selection be based largely on qualifications of personality and temperament, or on other characteristics? Is there any training which might be useful for the job other than on-the-job training?

7. Should the representative view his job as a stepping stone to top management positions or as a staff job in which long tenure for an indefinite time makes for greater effectiveness?

8. What recommendations would the representative make for increasing his effectiveness on behalf of the company? To whom in the company should the representative report?

SESSION 7

The Use of Groups and Specialists

1. Business and trade groups
   a. Types of groups (and examples of each):
      (1) General business—National Association of Manufacturers, U.S. Chamber of Commerce, etc.
      (2) Special business—National Security Industrial Association, American Ordnance Association, Navy League, National Small Business Men's Association, etc.
      (3) General trade associations—American Iron and Steel, American Petroleum, Aircraft Industries, etc.
      (4) Regional and special trade associations—Mid-Continent Oil and Gas, Scrap Iron and Steel Institute, etc.
   b. What dealings does the representative have with each of the above types of groups? In what kinds of situation are they useful? In what kinds of situation can the representative be useful to the groups?
   c. What problems do these groups create for the representative?
   d. How competent are the personnel of these groups? How effective are the various types of groups in:
      (1) Sales activity
      (2) Executive agency problems
      (3) Legislative problems
      (4) Alerting companies that do not maintain representatives.
   e. To what extent are the activities of these groups competitive with those of the representative?
   f. What steps would the representative recommend to his company in terms of membership in, and use of, groups to increase their effectiveness?

2. Specialists on Washington problems
   a. Types of specialists:
      (1) General counsel (Washington).
      (2) Legislative counsel and lobbyists.
      (3) Public relations counsel (Washington).
      (4) Management counsel.
      (5) Other.
   b. To what extent do the duties of the representative cause him or his company to seek the assistance of outside specialists? Under what circumstances? On what kind of problem?

c. What are the relationships and differences between outside specialists and specialists in the company?

d. Does the representative typically direct the efforts of such specialists or is this done by others in the company? What kind of latitude is the specialist given as to both strategy and tactics?

e. What are the advantages and disadvantages of using specialists as the representative sees it? To what extent do these specialists "compete" with the representative?

f. How could specialists be more effective and be more effectively used?

SESSION 8

Conclusion

1. Basic and applied research
   a. Have we covered adequately the role of the representative and his staff in serving as a bridge between his company and the government in both basic and applied research? Is this an important area of responsibility? How is it handled?

2. Business and political activity
   a. What type of policy, if any, should a company have with respect to the political interest and activity of its employees and supervisors?
      (1) No policy.
      (2) Company policy of encouraging all of its employees to take an active interest in political issues and participate in political activity, regardless of party.
      (3) Company policy of encouraging only its management and supervisory personnel to take an active interest in political issues and participate in political activity, regardless of party?
      (4) Same as (1) above, but top officials let it be known that they strongly believe in one or another party and work for this party.
      (5) Company policy of encouraging employees or supervisory personnel to participate in the activities of a particular party.
      (6) Other polices.
   b. How far should the corporation itself go in becoming politically more active? What are the advantages? Disadvantages?
   c. How far should top officials go in getting into political activity—bipartisan or single party?
      (1) Encouraging good candidates to run.
      (2) Campaign contributions.

(3) Assisting in campaign.

(4) Furnishing advice or services to elected official.

3. Strengthening the function of the Washington representative

a. To what extent is the strengthening of the function within the control of the representative and to what extent dependent on the company's giving permission or furnishing resources?

b. What steps are the participants now contemplating aimed at strengthening their function that can be taken without the permission of the company or without any substantial assistance from the company?

c. If the management of their companies asked the participants to recommend three things that they could do that would improve their ability to do a more effective job of representing the companies in Washington, what would they be?

4. Assistance to the government

a. It is apparent that the representative spends some of his time in giving assistance or advice to the government, almost wholly unrelated to direct company interests. How much time is involved? On what kinds of problems, committees, panels, etc.?

5. The Washington representative a decade from now

a. What will the job of the Washington representative be in ten years? How will it differ from the job today?

b. What are the basic trends in government, business, and business-government relations that indicate the answer to the preceding question?

c. Will more companies have representatives in ten years?

d. What will be the relationship of the representative to business groups and specialists a decade from now.